Ford Madox Ford

THE SOUL
OF LONDON
A Survey of a Modern City

'A Traveller? By my faith you have
great reason to be sad!'*

Edited by
ALAN G. HILL
Royal Holloway, University of London

EVERYMAN
J. M. DENT · LONDON
CHARLES E. TUTTLE
VERMONT

Introduction and other critical apparatus © J. M. Dent 1995

First published in Everyman in 1995

Reprinted 1998

J. M. Dent
Orion Publishing Group
Orion House
5 Upper St Martin's Lane
London WC2H 9EA
and
Charles E. Tuttle Co. Inc.
28 South Main Street
Rutland, Vermont 05701, USA

Typeset by CentraCet Limited, Cambridge
Printed and bound in Great Britain by
The Guernsey Press Co. Ltd, Guernsey, C.I.

British Library Cataloguing-in-Publication Data is available
upon request.

ISBN 0 460 87621 X

Everyman, I will go with thee,
and be thy guide

THE EVERYMAN
LIBRARY

*The Everyman Library was founded by J. M. Dent
in 1906. He chose the name Everyman because he wanted
to make available the best books ever written in every
field to the greatest number of people at the cheapest possible
price. He began with Boswell's 'Life of Johnson';
his one-thousandth title was Aristotle's 'Metaphysics',
by which time sales exceeded forty million.*

*Today Everyman paperbacks remain true to
J. M. Dent's aims and high standards, with a wide range
of titles at affordable prices in editions which address
the needs of today's readers. Each new text is reset to give
a clear, elegant page and to incorporate the latest thinking
and scholarship. Each book carries the pilgrim logo,
the character in 'Everyman', a medieval mystery play,
a proud link between Everyman
past and present.*

CONTENTS

THE SOUL OF LONDON

INTRODUCTORY 3

Chapter 1 FROM A DISTANCE 7

No mental image of London from a distance – 'He knows his London' –
What he knows – The born Londoner – The provincial immigrant – His
preconceptions – His aloneness – His induction – He becomes the
Londoner – London, an abstraction – Its forgetfulness – Its tolerance – Its
assimilative powers – London, a permanent World's Fair – Mental images
of former Londoners – London illimitable – Trafalgar Square – A horse
down – The Saturday-night market – Class views – What the Londoner
sees from afar – The foreigner's view of London – The Londoner
confronted with this view – Its effect on him – His ignorance of London –
London, a background – What we remember of London – London
manifesting itself on the clouds

Chapter 2 ROADS INTO LONDON 25

Where the country ends – The three Londons – The psychological – The
Administrative County – Natural London – The ring of blackened tree
trunks – Elms – The new carriages – Entering on a motor car – Its effects
on the mind – Distances to be thought of in new terms – Entering on an
electric tram – The possibility of looking round – A manifestation of the
modern spirit – The electric tram at night – Its romantic appearance –

Chapter 5 REST IN LONDON   93

The cloisters of our Valhalla – The unknown author – The waste of
individualities – The pleasantest size for a graveyard – The cemetery –
Athens versus Kensington High Street – The Londoner – The impossibility
of finding him – The death of the Spirit of Place – The individualist and his
neighbours – At Père-la-Chaise – The discussion in the cloisters – The
school boys – The disappearance of the great figure – Spring clouds – The
forgotten hills – The stern reformer – Building improvements – 'History'
ends with the young Pretender – The beginning of 'movements' – The ideal
city of the reformer – The end of furniture – Utopia – The alternative –
The end of London – The elements – The charity school – The garden
plots – The Monastic reformers – 'That neurasthenia joke' – The sick farm
labourer – A race that will survive – London from a distance – The cloud

NOTE ON THE AUTHOR AND EDITOR

FORD MADOX FORD (or Hueffer as he was first known) was born in 1873, son of Francis Hueffer the German Wagnerian scholar and grandson of Ford Madox Brown the painter, and he grew up in Pre-Raphaelite circles in London. Following a fruitful period of collaboration with Joseph Conrad, he scored his first success with a prophetic survey of modern life, *The Soul of London* (1905). This was followed by the three *Fifth Queen* novels (1906–8), which Conrad called 'the swan song of historical romance'. Ford's technical virtuosity was perfected in *The Good Soldier* (1915), in which all his preoccupations as a novelist came together for the first time.

He was less successful in managing his private life, which was punctuated by scandal and threats of litigation, and after active service at the Front during the First World War, he never settled permanently in England again, moving for the rest of his life between Paris, Provence and America, where his work was better known than in his own country. His masterpiece, the four novels that make up *Parade's End*, appeared between 1924 and 1928.

Poet and critic as well as a brilliant editor and promoter of the talents of others, Ford spread his gifts unevenly over more than eighty books, many of them unread today; but he remained to the end (as he said) 'an old man mad about writing', though largely ignored by the English literary establishment. Ford Madox Ford died at Deauville in 1939, on the eve of the Second World War.

ALAN G. HILL is Professor of English in London University (Royal Holloway College), and General Editor of *The Letters of William and Dorothy Wordsworth* (Oxford University Press, 8 vols, 1967–93). He has written extensively on the literature and ideas of the Romantics and Victorians.

CHRONOLOGY OF FORD'S LIFE

Year	Age	Life
1873		Born 17 December at Merton, Surrey, the eldest of the three children of Francis Hueffer, music critic, and Catherine Brown, daughter of Ford Madox Brown, the artist. Ford retains surname Hueffer till 1919
1874–80		The family moves to Brook Green, Hammersmith, seeing much of Brown and his friends at Fitzroy Square. Ford's childhood spent in literary and Pre-Raphaelite circles
1881–8		At boarding school in Folkestone. First of many visits to Germany
1889	16	On father's death the family move to Brown's house near Regent's Park. Ford briefly at University College School
1890–1	18	Moving in Fabian, Aesthetic and literary circles, and exploring the London scene

CHRONOLOGY OF HIS TIMES

Year	Cultural Context	Historical Events
1873	Pater, *Studies in the History of the Renaissance*	Gladstone Prime Minister
1874	Francis Hueffer, *Wagner and the Music of the Future* Sisley, *Weir at Molesey*	Disraeli Prime Minister. First Impressionist Exhibition in Paris. Bicycle invented
1875	Swinburne, *Songs of Two Nations* Whistler, *Nocturne in Blue and Gold*	Telephone invented. Society of French Artists' Exhibition in London
1880	Deaths of George Eliot and Flaubert	Gladstone Prime Minister
1881	Death of Carlyle James, *The Portrait of a Lady*	Married Women's Property Act
1883	Deaths of Wagner and Turgenev Maupassant, *Une Vie*	
1885	Jefferies, *After London* Birth of Pound	Radio waves discovered; internal combustion engine invented
1888	Birth of T. S. Eliot Maupassant, *Pierre et Jean* Early works of Kipling and Yeats	
1889	Charles Booth, *Life and Labour of the People in London* (completed 1903)	
1890	William James, *Principles of Psychology*	First underground electric railway in London
1891	Morris, *News from Nowhere* Hardy, *Tess of the D'Urbervilles* Gissing, *New Grub Street*	

Year	Age	Life
1892	19	Received into Roman Catholic Church during a visit to Hueffer relatives in Paris
1894	20	After earlier volumes of poems and fairy tales, publishes his first novel *The Shifting of the Fire*. (May) runaway marriage to Elsie Martindale; they settle in rural Kent
1896	23	Publishes biography of his grandfather, F. M. Brown (d.1893)
1898	25	Meets Joseph Conrad: their collaboration produces *The Inheritors* (1901) and *Romance* (1903). In due course also gets to know Wells, Crane, Galsworthy, Hudson and Henry James
1900	27	*The Cinque Ports* published
1902	29	Publishes study of Dante Gabriel Rossetti to whom he was related on his mother's side
1903	30	(Feb.) begins *The Soul of London*
1904	31	(Mar.) finishes *The Soul of London*. Illness and nervous collapse. Writes life of Holbein at Basle (published 1905)
1905	32	*The Soul of London* published. (Later sequels: *The Heart of the Country*, 1906; and *The Spirit of the People*, 1907; all 3 parts published in America as *England and the English*, 1907). *The Benefactor* published

Year	Cultural Context	Historical Events
1895	Hardy, *Jude the Obscure* Crane, *Red Badge of Courage*	X-rays discovered
1896	Death of William Morris Morrison, *A Child of the Jago*	Wireless telegraphy invented
1899	Conrad, *Heart of Darkness* serialized (published 1902) Besant, *South London* Delius, *Paris, the Song of a* *Great City*	Boer War begins (ends 1902)
1900	Deaths of Ruskin and Wilde Symons, *The Symbolist* *Movement in Literature* Wells, *Love and Mr Lewisham* Dreiser, *Sister Carrie* Freud, *The Interpretation of* *Dreams*	British Labour Party founded
1901	Kipling, *Kim* Mann, *Buddenbrooks* Elgar, *Cockaigne Overture*	Death of Queen Victoria; accession of Edward VII
1903	Death of Whistler James, *The Ambassadors* Norris, *The Pit* Shaw, *Man and Superman*	Balfour Prime Minister (1902–5). First aeroplane flight
1904	Conrad, *Nostromo* Hudson, *Green Mansions* Hardy, Part I of *The Dynasts*	Rutherford discovers radioactivity
1905	James, *The Golden Bowl* Shaw, *Major Barbara* (published 1907) Wells, *Kipps*	Einstein's special theory of relativity. Suffragist agitation begins

Year	Age	Life
1906	33	First visit to America; meets Willa Cather. *The Fifth Queen*, the first of the Katharine Howard trilogy, published. (*Privy Seal* published 1907; *The Fifth Queen Crowned* published 1908)
1907	34	*An English Girl* published
1908	35	Affair with Violet Hunt begins. Founds *English Review*, with contributions from Hardy, Lawrence, Yeats, James, Forster
1910	37	*A Call* published
1911	38	*Ancient Lights* (reminiscences), *The Critical Attitude*, and *Ladies Whose Bright Eyes* published. Elsie refuses to divorce Ford: the scandal, and libel action that follows, lead to Ford's ostracism from society
1913	40	*Collected Poems* published
1915	42	*The Good Soldier* and *When Blood is Their Argument* published. Enlists in army
1916	43	Sent out to the Front and sees active service on the Somme
1918	45	Breaks with Violet Hunt as the war ends
1919	46	Settles with Stella Bowen in West Sussex to cultivate the land
1922	49	Moves to Paris and the Riviera
1923	50	Starts *Transatlantic Review* in Paris, publishing Hemingway, Pound, Joyce, Eliot

Year	Cultural Context	Historical Events
1906	Sinclair, *The Jungle*	
1907	Birth of Auden Conrad, *The Secret Agent* Bergson, *L'Evolution Créatrice*	
1908	Symons, *London, A Book of Aspects* Forster, *A Room with a View* Pound, *Personae*	Asquith Prime Minister. Old Age Pensions Act
1909	Wells, *Tono Bungay*	
1910		Death of Edward VII; accession of George V
1911	Pound, *Canzoni*	National Insurance Act
1913	Lawrence, *Sons and Lovers* Proust, *Swann's Way* Sickert, first version of *Ennui*	
1914	Joyce, *Dubliners* (completed 1905) Lewis, *Blast* Vaughan Williams, *London Symphony*	(Aug.) Beginning of First World War
1915	Woolf, *The Voyage Out* Richardson, *Pointed Roofs*	Second battle of Ypres
1916	Death of Henry James Joyce, *Portrait of the Artist as a Young Man*	First battle of the Somme. Lloyd George Prime Minister
1917	Eliot, *Prufrock and Other Observations*	Battle of Passchendaele. Russian Revolution
1918	Willa Cather, *My Antonia*	(Nov.) Armistice with Germany. Votes for Women over 30
1919	Anderson, *Winesburg, Ohio*	Treaty of Versailles
1922	Eliot, *The Waste Land* Joyce, *Ulysses* Sinclair Lewis, *Babbit*	Fascist government in Italy. Women given equality in divorce proceedings

Year	Age	Life
1924	51	*Joseph Conrad, A Personal Reminiscence*, and *Some Do Not* published, the first of the Tietjens tetralogy, later entitled *Parade's End*. (*No More Parades*, 1925; *A Man Could Stand Up*, 1926; *Last Post*, 1928)
1926–38		Moves between France and America for the rest of his life
1927	54	Separates from Stella Bowen
1929	56	*The English Novel* published
1930	57	Settles with Janice Biala in Provence
1931	58	*Return to Yesterday* published (reminiscences up to 1914)
1933	60	*It Was the Nightingale* (reminiscences after 1918), and *The Rash Act* published
1935	62	*Provence* published
1937	64	*Great Trade Route*. Teaching at Olivet College, Michigan
1938	65	Hon. D. Litt. Olivet College. *The March of Literature* published
1939	65	Returns to France. (26 June) Dies at Deauville

Year	Cultural Context	Historical Events
1924	Deaths of Conrad and Kafka (*The Trial* published 1925) Forster, *A Passage to India*	First Labour government under Ramsay MacDonald. Death of Lenin
1925	Woolf, *Mrs Dalloway* Pound, *16 Cantos* Dreiser, *An American Tragedy* Fitzgerald, *The Great Gatsby*	
1926	Hemingway, *The Sun Also Rises*	General Strike
1927	Woolf, *To the Lighthouse* Cather, *Death Comes for the Archbishop* Proust completes *A la Recherche du Temps Perdu*	
1929	Hemingway, *A Farewell to Arms*	
1930	Auden, *Poems* Hart Crane, *The Bridge*	World economic depression
1931	Woolf, *The Waves*	National Government formed
1933	Yeats, *Collected Poems*	Hitler becomes German Chancellor
1934	William Carlos Williams, *Collected Poems*	
1935	Wallace Stevens, *Ideas of Order* Steinbeck, *Tortilla Flat*	Baldwin Prime Minister for third time
1936	Auden and Isherwood, *The Ascent of F.6*	Abdication crisis. Outbreak of Spanish Civil War. F. D. Roosevelt begins second term as US President
1938	Cummings, *Collected Poems*	Chamberlain concludes Munich agreement
1939	Death of Yeats	(Sept.) Outbreak of Second World War

INTRODUCTION

Where, in the literature of the early twentieth century, do we find the clearest signs of those tendencies which have since been grouped together under the umbrella of Modernism? A reader might turn first to the early poems of Pound and T. S. Eliot written on the eve of the First World War, or to the early stories of Joseph Conrad from the previous decade, or even to William James's writings about the nature of human consciousness from even further back. But it could be argued that it is in *The Soul of London* (1905), this unassuming and neglected little work of Ford Madox Ford's, that one can detect in the most obvious way how literary concerns and priorities were changing in the new century. For all its old-fashioned title (which was suggested at a late stage by the publisher), *The Soul of London* stood out as a pointer to the future as soon as it began to take shape early in 1903. But it was also Ford's first really successful book, at a decisive moment in his development, and these are surely reasons enough why it should be better known and appreciated today.

From the time of Queen Victoria's Jubilee in 1877, London as a phenomenon of modern civilisation had been endlessly discussed in works of fact and fiction as it emerged from more than a century of unparalleled growth to outrival Chicago as the world city of the future. But if the magnificence of London was a theme for celebration, the city also had its underside, the squalor and human degradation which had cast a shadow over its prospects since the days of Dickens; and after the foundation of the London County Council in 1888 to reform local government in the capital, London and its problems were seldom out of the newspapers or the purview of more imaginative literature. Its history and topography were explored by Sir Walter Besant; Arthur Morrison depicted the unknown face of the East End; and Gissing and H. G. Wells made their mark with realistic novels of working-class life in the capital and its sprawling new suburbs. And there were many more works of literature exploring the 'facts' of London around the turn of the century.

In *The Soul of London*, however, Ford was writing a very different kind of book from any of his contemporaries, one in which 'impressions' took the place of information and argument, and the techniques of the novelist were applied to a mode of writing where they had rarely, if ever, been practised before. Ford's work belongs to no known category, though others like Arthur Symons, following the mood of Whistler's paintings, tried to imitate it in word pictures of the city. It also defies summary. Part history, part personal reminiscence, and partly a prose poem which renders 'the moods of many individuals' in relation to the urban landscape, *The Soul of London* reads at times like fiction, where the scene is set for characters who never actually appear. But, as the epigraph suggests, it is also a journey of discovery into the nature of modern city life and our ways of coming to terms with it. As such it is remarkably ahead of its time. 'The world is so full of a number of things', Ford was to write a little later in the *English Review*,

> facts so innumerably beset us, that the gatherer of facts is relatively of very little value. And when, each man by himself, we are seeking to make out the pattern of the bewildering carpet that modern life is, it matters very little whether the facts are those collected by the scientific historian, by the socio-political economist or by the collector of railroad statistics. But to be brought really into contact with our fellow men, to become intimately acquainted with the lives of those around us, this is a thing which grows daily more difficult in the complexities of modern life. This, vicariously, the artist is more and more needed to supply.

It is the challenge of modern urban society, with its sense of alienation and fragmentation, that gives the imaginative writer his fresh sense of purpose:

> . . . the tendency of humanity is to crowd into the large cities, and within their bounds to live semi-migratory lives. Of the history and of the thought of the great number of men with whom we come into contact we have no knowledge at all . . . Of their lives and passions we know nothing. So that unless the imaginative

writer help us in this matter we are in great danger of losing alike
human knowledge and human sympathy.

(Ford, *The Critical Attitude*, 1911, pp.66–7)

The old Romantic ideals had to be reasserted even more
urgently in this new situation. The province of literary art, Ford
claims, is 'the bringing of humanity into contact, person with
person' (as Wordsworth had maintained long before), and the
rejection of all factual detail which cramps the writer's vision
and keeps the ordinary reader at arm's length. How had Ford
come to see his role in these terms?

Ford, or Hueffer as he then was, had grown up in the
hothouse atmosphere of Pre-Raphaelitism, uncertain where his
true vocation lay, and dividing his time between music, art
criticism and literature without making very much of a success
of any of them. His reception into the Roman Catholic Church
had seemingly been dictated by deference to the German branch
of his family rather than his own inclinations; his runaway
marriage, while he was still under age, was the first of many
complications in his personal life that were periodically to
overwhelm him and confuse his sense of purpose; and even his
flirtation with Fabian socialism and the Arts and Crafts Movement bore the mark of the dilettante. Or as Henry James put it
more charitably in his portrait of Milton Densher, Ford
suggested

> that wondrous state of youth in which the elements, the metals
> more or less precious, are so in fusion and fermentation that the
> question of the final stamp, the pressure that fixes the final value,
> must wait for comparative coolness.
>
> (James, *The Wings of the Dove*, 1902, p. 55)

But all this changed after his meeting with Joseph Conrad in
1898. In the collaboration that followed – perhaps the most
remarkable in modern literature – Ford was converted whole-
heartedly to the Novel: not, however, to the English tradition of
Fielding and Thackeray, but to the art of Henry James and the
French and Russian masters, particularly Maupassant, whose
preface to *Pierre et Jean* (1888) had set out new aims for
practitioners of the craft of fiction.

The technique of 'impressionism' that emerged from Ford's
and Conrad's deliberations about the novelist's task was to

inform Ford's literary aims thereafter and transform his way of rendering the human scene in the masterpieces he was eventually to produce, his 'tale of passion' *The Good Soldier*, and the four parts of *Parade's End*, which render 'the public events of a decade' and the passing of an era. As in the analogous movement in French painting, the impressionist recognised that the relationship between writer and object was never a static one, but part of the flux of impressions that were passing through his mind at the moment of writing. The essence of reality was to be recaptured, not by factual completeness or authorial omniscience, but by a careful selection of telling details and visual effects projected spontaneously through the individual point of view of the writer. At its best, impressionism aims to *show* rather than to *explain*, but without tight imaginative control it can easily degenerate into garrulousness, as it tends to do in *The Heart of the Country* and *The Spirit of the People*, Ford's two sequels to *The Soul of London*. It can also be so allusive as to become downright obscure or careless of accuracy, faults from which *The Soul of London* is not entirely immune. The editor has his work cut out giving the minimum of explanation without holding up the onward flow of the text.

Ford was to set out his procedures at length in his 'personal remembrance' of *Joseph Conrad* (1924), and the details need not be repeated here: it is enough to say that *The Soul of London* was the first fruit of a technique that was soon to be extended to *The Fifth Queen* trilogy of historical romances, and eventually deployed to superb effect in the Armistice Day scene at the close of the third part of *Parade's End*. Ford had at last outgrown his Victorian roots and had found an engrossing artistic purpose. He was now launched on the first stage of his ambition to become the historian of his own times and (eventually) the heir of Proust.

Ford's introduction to *The Soul of London* is really a manifesto for the new method of rendering the appearance of the city as it is filtered through the artist's consciousness, – and he is supremely confident that he is creating a work of art and not a guidebook. In recapturing the atmosphere of modern London and the tide of humanity that flows through it, he aims to create a 'personal image of the place', and to 'render the actual' while avoiding sentiment and picturesque detail. The ideal author (that is, Ford himself) must be 'passionately alive to all aspects of life'.

> He must not only sniff at the 'Suburbs' as a place of small houses
> and dreary lives; he must remember that in each of these houses
> dwells a strongly individualised human being with romantic hopes,
> romantic fears, and at the end, an always tragic death.

The work evokes a picture of the bewildering variety of London life. But insofar as it is unified round certain recurring 'notes' of the Modern Spirit, a musical analogy is also suggested. Exponents of the symphonic poem were at this period turning to depict in musical terms the life of great cities, and it was not for nothing that Ford's father was the leading Wagnerian in Britain at this time.

The Soul of London will make a special appeal to all Londoners because it embodies so many experiences and feelings that they will recognise as exactly their own. It has never dated. Ford has an uncanny sense of the patchwork of attitudes and assumptions that form the psychology of the city-dweller and immigrant and the means whereby they make the metropolis *their own world* and the focus of all their hopes. Every page projects the excitement and challenge of London as 'the high watermark of achievement of the Modern Spirit', the world city, the child of all the ages, a permanent world's fair, and a magnet to which all humanity is irresistibly drawn. But Ford's stance is deeply ambivalent. For London is also 'a gigantic pantheon of the dead level of democracy . . . a home neither for the living nor the dead'. It swallows up all comers pitilessly. Its prevailing note is one of loneliness and anonymity. If London has any underlying harmony, it eludes analysis. The city can only be treated as 'a ground base, a drone, on top of which one pipes one's own small individual melody'. It offers therefore an incomparable backcloth for the small-scale dramas of modern life, – and here Ford anticipates the modern writer's preoccupation with *ennui* and *angst*, years before the publication of Joyce's *Dubliners* and Eliot's *Prufrock*.

> A man may look down out of dim windows upon the slaty, black,
> wet misery of a squalid street, upon a solitary, hurrying passer's
> umbrella. He may have received a moment before the first embrace
> of a woman, or a moment before his doctor may have told him

that he is not very long for this world. He will stand looking down; and a sudden consonance with his mood ... a sudden significance will be there in the black wet street, in the long wavering reflections on the gleaming paving-stones, in the engrossed hurry of the passer-by.

At the close of the first section, Ford's apocalyptic vision of London, a direct reminiscence of Conrad's *Heart of Darkness* which had just appeared, is alluring but ominous:

Viewed from a distance it is a cloud on the horizon. From the dark, further side of the Surrey hills at night, above the inky skyline of heather, of pine tops, of elms, one may see on the sky a brooding and sinister glow. That is London – manifesting itself on the clouds.

Contrary to popular belief, London is not a stable entity at all, but a phantasmagoria of shifting scenes and impressions; and in his second section, 'Roads into London', Ford turns to the changing face of the city, the contrasts of urban decay and modern 'improvements', the jumble of half-finished streets, jerry-built terraces, and speculative building, where nothing seems fixed and permanent. Can Progress be meaningful amid such a turmoil of unrelated and incompatible aims, or is it just a romantic illusion? These pages are full of unforgettable pictures of journeys across London by day and night, by barge, in horse-drawn buses or electric trams, or by market wagons, and arresting scenes like the marshalling yards at night, – or this disconcerting vision of a London dawn:

All the empty streets giving out echoes that one never hears during the day, all the vacant blinds, the sinister, the jocular, the lugubriously inquiring, or the lamentable expressions that windows give to houses asleep, all the smoking chimneys, the pale skies, and the thought of all these countless thousands lying invisible, with their souls, in sleep, parted from their bodies – all these things give an effect, in its silence, immense, stealthy, and overpowering.

Life as we now experience it is fragmented, incomplete, like the random events observed from a train window as we are propelled through the suburbs:

I looked down upon black and tiny yards that were like the cells
in an electric battery. In one, three children were waving their
hands and turning up white faces to the train; in the next white
clothes were drying. A little further on a woman ran suddenly out
of a door ... A man followed her hastily ... in his hand a long
stick. We moved on, and I have not the least idea whether he was
going to thrash her, or whether together they were going to beat a
carpet.

This kind of experience will be familiar to every commuter
today. It is part of the pathos and dissatisfaction of modern
living that it no longer satisfies 'the sentiment ingrained in
humanity of liking a story to have an end.' It was a consolation
that twentieth-century novelists were increasingly to deny to
their readers.

What place can there be in the modern city for the vital
human needs of work and play? In the two central sections of
The Soul of London we approach the heart of Ford's
impressions of modern civilisation of which we have only had
glimpses so far. If London is a magnet to all comers, it is like a
vast gaming table or battlefield after they arrive, an arena for
the desperate struggle of George Bernard Shaw's and Bergson's
Life Force. Man has become a cog in an impersonal machine,
and mass production has turned individual effort into a round
of monotonous and repetitive tasks of the kind which Chaplin
was to caricature years later in his film 'Modern Times'. The
streets of London may be paved with gold, but only the ruthless
Napoleons of industry can survive there; and no employment
may be available for the artist except as an office worker (a
prophecy of Ford's that was to be fulfilled in the careers of T. S.
Eliot, Wallace Stevens and the composer Charles Ives). The
working man's creativity passes into hobbies like pigeon-fancy-
ing, a poignant reminder of the rural society he has left behind.
As an inarticulate victim of the new entrepreneurs and their
ever-changing industrial processes (not to mention the waste
land they leave behind), the worker fares no better under the
new corporations and public authorities; but at least he or she
has a predestined niche in the system – like the matchbox-
maker, perhaps the most striking of Ford's epiphanies of the
London poor who stoically accept their fate and 'keep all on
going' in spite of social change and deprivation:

> You could not pity her because she was so obviously and wonderfully equipped for her particular struggle: you could not wish to 'raise' her, for what could she do in any other light, in any other air? Here at least she was strong, heroic, settled and beyond any condemnation.

Like Carlyle and Ruskin, and his early mentor William Morris, Ford is on the side of the craftsmen and small producers against the monopolists and collectivists. He has every sympathy for the displaced countrymen and gipsies who have survived from an earlier stage of society. But the romance of London finally disarms all criticism, because it presents so human a face to the world.

The leisured classes are preserved from the meaningless drudgery of the workers, but their days are just as devoid of meaning, for all the glamour and excitement of their life-style. They have no tasks to give shape to their existence. Ford paints a devastating picture of the trivial pursuits of their average day:

> You carry away from it a vague kaleidoscopic picture – lights in clusters, the bare shoulders of women, white flannel on green turf in the sunlight, darkened drawing rooms with nasal voices chanting parodies of prayers, the up and down strokes of fiddle bows, the flicker of fifty couples whirling round before you as with a touch of headache you stood in a doorway, a vague recollection of a brilliant anecdote, the fag end of a conversation beneath the palms of a dimmed conservatory, and a fatigue and a feverish idea that if you had missed any one of these unimportant things you would have missed life.

It is only by retreat from this empty social round into the depths of solitude which only a vast city can offer, that the artist can have his own precious moments of illumination:

> So Time becomes manifest like a slow pulse, the world stands still; a four-wheeler takes as it were two years to crawl from one lamp-post to another, and the rustle of newspapers behind your back in the dark recesses of the room might be a tide chafing upon the pebbles. That is your deep and blessed leisure: the pause in the beat of the clock that comes now and then to make life seem worth going on with.

But the consolations of the artistic life depend on a writer's contact with 'the spell of contagious humanity', and this is often denied him in the cultural malaise of modern society. Reading is out of date, apart from the newspapers, social contacts are minimal (and confined to team games and public courtship rituals), and even neighbours are a thing of the past. This is 'the level mediocrity of democracy', as Auden was later to recapture it in *The Ascent of F.6* in all its drab uniformity:

> The old old story that never ends:
> The eight o'clock train, the customary place,
> Holding the paper in front of your face,
> The public stairs, the glass swing-door,
> The peg for your hat, the linoleum floor . . .

– the boredom and sheer predictability of the daily routine. What future is there for the artist when he can no longer depend on a community of like-minded readers? It is as if, in the act of evoking this world, the writer may be signing his own death warrant.

In drawing together his impressions in the book's last section, Ford returns to his earlier apocalyptic manner as he takes a longer view of London 'at rest' and the countless generations that have given their lives to its making:

> And what is London but a vast graveyard of stilled hopes in which the thin gnats-swarm of the present population dances its short day above the daily growing, indisturbable detritus of all the past at rest?

Man is dwarfed into insignificance in this vast necropolis of dead hopes and futile endeavours. 'What is one generation of the living compared to the innumerable generations of the dead?' Yet the spirit of humanity is unquenchable, though London as a place may be soulless. History is made up of people, not forces. 'To destroy these individualities is impossible.' The hope for the future must lie in what Ford calls 'the apotheosis of modern life', the raising of mankind to new heights in the evolutionary process. Evolution, apparently so careless of the individual, may yet throw up a 'town type' which is more fitted to survive and prosper than the present inhabitants of London. But there can be no certainty in these matters. Civic order and public health may meantime break down, and then London will revert to the primeval swamps from which it originally rose (and here there is another reminiscence of Conrad's *Heart of Darkness*). As a portent of the way modern civilisation is going, the 'brooding and enigmatic glow' of London on the night sky remains deeply ambiguous; but thanks to Ford's faith in humanity and the artistry and verve of his projection of the London scene, *The Soul of London* is not as a whole gloomy or pessimistic, unlike so many other works that had appeared at the close of the nineteenth century.

In *The Soul of London* and its two sequels Ford had at last found a fruitful direction for his talents in surveying the early twentieth century world which was to become the theatre for his fictions. He had also foreshadowed the way in which his vision was to progress. The story of his further development, both in technique and knowledge of life, and the major novels that came out of it, need not concern us here. It is enough to say that in finding his own métier he thereby helped to define the territory, tone and procedures of much of the literature of the new century. To have attempted all this, and at the same time created an engaging work of lasting interest, is surely a notable achievement, and justifies the republication of the work for a new generation of readers.

ALAN G. HILL

NOTE ON THE TEXT

This edition of *The Soul of London* follows the text of the first edition (London: Alston Rivers, 1905), but a few misprints have been silently corrected. *The Soul of London* was reissued by Duckworth and Co. in 1911, as part of the *Readers' Library*, but apparently without a full correction of the text.

THE SOUL OF LONDON

INTRODUCTORY

Most of us love places very much as we may love what, for us, are the distinguished men of our social lives. Paying a visit to such a man we give, in one form or another, our impressions to our friends: since it is human to desire to leave some memorial that shall record our view of the man at the stage he has reached. We describe his manners, his shape, his utterances: we moralise a little about his associates, his ethics, the cut of his clothes; we relate gossip about his past before we knew him, or we predict his future when we shall be no more with him. We are, all of us who are Londoners, paying visits of greater or less duration to a Personality that, whether we love it or very cordially hate it, fascinates us all. And, paying my visit, I have desired to give some such record.

I have tried to make it anything rather than encyclopaedic, topographical, or archaeological. To use a phrase of literary slang I have tried to 'get the atmosphere' of modern London – of the town in which I have passed so many days; of the immense place that has been the background for so many momentous happenings to so many of my fellows.

A really ideal book of the kind would not contain 'writing about' a town: it would throw a personal image of the place on to the paper. It would not contain such a sentence as: 'There are in the city of — 720 firms of hat manufacturers employing 19,000 operatives.' Instead there would be a picture of one, or two, or three hat factories, peopled with human beings, where slow and clinging veils of steam waver over vats and over the warm felt on cutters' slabs. And there would be conveyed the idea that all these human beings melt, as it were, into the tide of humanity as all these vapours melt into the overcast skies.

Similarly, in touching upon moral ideas, a book about places must be passionate in its attempt after truth of rendering; it must be passionless in the deductions that it draws. It must let neither pity for the poor nor liking for established reputations and clean floors, warp its presentations where they bear, say, upon the Housing Question. Its business is to give a picture of the place as its author sees it; its reader must seek in other books, statistics, emotional views, or facts handy for political propaganda.

This author's treatment of historic matters must again be 'presentations'; and he must select only such broad tendencies, or such minute historic characters as bear straight upon some aspect of his subject. The historic facts must illustrate, must cast a light upon modern London, if that is what is being presented. There must be no writing about Dr Johnson's chair* in a certain tavern merely because it appeals to the author. The reader will find details of all such things in other books – this author's endeavour should be to make the Past, the sense of all the dead Londons that have gone to the producing of this child of all the ages, like a constant ground-bass beneath the higher notes of the Present. In that way the book might, after a fashion, forecast even the Future and contain prophecies. It should, in fact, be instinct with the Historic sense which will afford apt illustrations, rather than the annalist's industry, or the love of the picturesque.

That sense of the picturesque will, however, be both a salvation and a most dangerous stumbling-block. In a turning off an opulent High Street, there is a court with the exterior aspect of which I am very familiar. It is close to a large freestone Town Hall and to a very tall red-brick Fire Station. It is entered by a square archway through which you get a glimpse of dazzlingly white cottages that, very obviously, were once thatched, but that now have pretty red tiles. It is flagged with very large, old stones. It is as picturesque as you can imagine; it is a 'good thing' for descriptive writing, it might be legitimate to use it. But the trouble is that it is old – and, if the book were all old things, deluding by a love for the picturesque of antiquity, it would give a very false and a very sentimental rendering of London.

But the author might desire to illustrate the tendency of parasitic humanity to lurk in the shadow of wealthy High Streets. – This court would be an excellent illustration: it is peopled with 'bad characters', male and female. Or he might desire to illustrate the economic proposition that letting small houses to bad characters is more profitable than selling the land for the erection of flats. – Hence, again, the court, would be an illustration; its extreme cleanliness, neatness and good repair would go to prove how careful that landlord was to prevent the condemnation of his rookery on sanitary grounds.

The author then must be careful not to sentimentalise over the picturesque. His business is to render the actual. His heart may be – it ought to be – torn at the sight of great boardings, raised for the house-breakers, round narrow courts, old streets, famous houses. He ought to be alive to the glamour of old associations, of all the old associations in all their human aspects. – But he ought to be equally inspired with satisfaction because work is being done; because dark spots are being cleared away; because new haunts are being formed for new people around whom will congregate new associations. And he ought to see that these new associations will in their turn grow old, tender, romantic, glamorous enough. He should, in fact, when he presumes to draw morals, be prepared to draw all the morals. – He must not only sniff at the 'Suburbs' as a place of small houses and dreary lives; he must remember that in each of these houses dwells a strongly individualised human being with romantic hopes, romantic fears, and at the end, an always tragic death. He must remember that the thatched, mud-hovels that crowded round the Tower* of original London, were just as dull, just as ordinary, just as commonplace; that men in them lived lives, according to their scale, just as squalid and just as unromantic – or just as alert and just as tragic. This author – this ideal author – then, must be passionately alive to all aspects of life. What picturesqueness there is in his work must arise from contrasts – but actual contracts vividly presented. This is what gives interest to a work of art; and such a work must, before all things, be interesting.

It is along these lines that I have tried to work: one falls, no doubt very far short of one's ideal. But, for my own part, if this particular work gives a number of readers pleasure or that counterpart of pleasure which is pain; if it awakens a Londoner here or there to an interest in the human aspects of his London; or if a man who loves London here and there throughout the world and across many seas is aroused to a bitter sweet remembering of old days, if in fact its note rings true to a section of mankind, I should call myself satisfied.

I should like, if it can be done unobtrusively, to disarm

criticism of the title of this book. It appears pretentious; it appears 'soul-ful'; it does little to indicate the scope of the book. But alas! If the critic will read the Table of Contents, and will then think for a minute or so of what one word will describe this whole hotchpotch, he will, whilst condemning, drop something like a tear for one who has been trying to find a better title, not for a minute or so, but for many months.

CHAPTER I

From a Distance

I

Thought of from sufficiently far, London offers to the mind's eye singularly little of a picture. It is essentially 'town', and yet how little of a town, how much of an abstraction. One says, 'He knows his London', yet how little more will he know of London than what is actually 'his'. And, if by chance he were an astronomer, how much better he might know his solar system.

It remains in the end always a matter of approaches. He has entered it – your man who knows his London – in one or other more or less strongly featured quarter; in his Bloomsbury of dismal, decorous, unhappy, glamorous squares; in his Camden Town of grimy box-like houses, yellow gas and perpetual ring of tram-horse hoofs; his eyes have opened to it in his Kensington, his Hoxton, his Mayfair or his Shoreditch. He has been born in it, or he has been drawn into it; he has gone through in it the slow awakening of a childhood. Or, coming an adolescent, his eyes have been opened more or less swiftly, with more or less of a wrench, to that small portion of it that is afterwards to form a 'jumping-off place' into that London that he will make 'his'.

And, with its 'atmosphere' whatever it is, with its 'character' whatever it may be, with the odd touches that go to make up familiarity and the home-feeling, the shape of its policemen's helmets, the cachet of its shop fronts, effects of light cast by steel lamps on the fog, on house fronts, on front garden trees, on park railings, all these little things going towards its atmosphere and character, that jumping-off place will remain for him, as it were, a glass through which he will afterwards view, a standard by which he will afterwards measure, the London that yet remains no one's.

It makes in essentials little enough difference whether he be born in a London quarter, or whether he came, a young provincial, raw and ready to quiver at every sensation, super-sensitized to every emotion. If, as a London child, he have wandered much in the streets, there will remain to him always an odd sensation of being very little, of peering round the corners of gray and gigantic buildings upon grayer vistas of buildings more gigantic – so, with a half touch of awe, we scramble, as relatively little in maturity, round the base of an out-jutting cliff into what may prove a gray cove or what may be a great bay. It is the sense of making discoveries, of a world's opening-up.

In both, at the start, there will be the essential provincialism. The London child, with his unconscious acknowledgement of impersonal vistas, of infinite miles of unmeaning streets, of horizons that are the blur of lamps in fogs, simultaneously acknowledges personalities, local oddities, local celebrities of whom Shepherd's Bush, Highgate or Knightsbridge may be proud. For the provincial adolescent there will be the Squire with his long beard and gouty walk, the Mayor with his shop in the High Street, the Doctor with his face screwed up as if he were tasting the full bitterness of one of his own potions. The London child, however, will earlier overcome his awe of person-alities. He will wonder at the man, sallow, tiny, wizened and skew-featured, who, with the whispered reputation of a miser able to roll himself in sovereigns, and a hazy identity in a child's mind with, say, Sweeny Todd the Demon Barber,* sells him spring-pistols,* catapult elastic and alley-taws* in the dim and evil light of a small shop with windows obscured by broad-sheets and penny dreadfuls. He will attach a certain significance to the grimy stretch of waste ground – it will by now have been, ah, so long since 'built over' – on which he played cricket with meat tins for a wicket, or fought a dismal battle with a big boy from 'another school'. But these local feelings sink very soon into the solid background of memories. He will discover other catapult sellers, he will find playing fields larger and more green, he will have it brought home to him that there are so many of every sort of thing in the world, just as, sooner or later, it will come home to him that there are so very many others of as little import in the scale of things as the catapult seller, the green fields, – and as himself.

For, sooner or later, the sense of the impersonality, of the abstraction that London is, will become one of the most intimate factors of his daily life. And sooner rather than later it will become one for the young provincial.

He will have had his preconceptions: he will have seen photographs of 'bits', of buildings, of bridges. He will have had his vague idea of a bulbous domed St Paul's with a queer fragment of Ludgate Hill, standing isolated at a corner of the Green Park; of Nelson's Column and the Monument,* of the Houses of Parliament and Buckingham Palace – all hazily united into one 'view' by a river Thames that is hazily suggested, green and leafy, by his own Severn, his own Stour, his own Ouse, or Adur.* But this picture will vanish finally and irrecoverably, like our own preconceived notions of an individual we have long thought of, whom we meet at last to find so entirely – and so very obviously – different.

The emotions of his journey to town – and they are emotions from within so much more than impressions from without – will last him until he is settled, more or less, for good in his lodgings, his cellar or his boarding house. They will last him, at least until his things are unpacked, his credentials presented, his place found – or until he finds, after how many disillusionments, that he may never in all probability find any place at all. The point is that, till then, he will not have any time to 'look about him'.

2

But the last thing that, even then, he will get is any picture, any impresson of London as a whole, any idea to carry about with him – of a city, in a plain, dominated by a great building, bounded by a horizon, brought into composition by mists, great shadows, great clouds or a bright and stippled foreground. It is trite enough to say that the dominant note of his first impression will be that of his own alone-ness. It is none the less the dominant note of London; because, unless he is actually alone he will pay no attention to London itself. He will talk with his companions of his or their own affairs; he will retain the personal note, shutting out the impersonal, stalling it off instinctively.

But our young Provincial being for his first time cast absolutely loose will get then his first impression of London – his first tap of the hammer. He will stand perhaps at a street corner, perhaps at his own doorstep, for a moment at a loss what to do, where to go, where to turn. He will not ever have been so alone. If he were intent upon getting a complete picture of London he might be – we might imagine him – setting out self-consciously, his eyes closed during the transit, to climb the heights of Hampstead, the top of the Monument, the Dome of St Paul's. But he will not.

London, with its sense of immensity that we must hurry through to keep unceasing appointments, with its diffuseness, its gatherings up into innumerable trade-centres, innumerable class districts, becomes by its immensity a place upon which there is no beginning. It is, so to speak, a ragoût of tit-bits so appealing and so innumerable – of Gower's tombs and Botticelli's,* of miles of port-wine cellars or of the waxen effigies* of distinguished murderers – that your actual born-not-made Londoner passes the whole dish by. He is like the good Scot whose haggis is only eaten by conscientious tourists; like the good North German whose *alt-bier* soup* appears at table only for the discomfiture of the English or American cousin. He will not visit his Tower today because there will always remain an eternity in which to see it; he will not, tomorrow, ensue at the Millbank National Gallery* a severe headache, because that Gallery will always be there.

Our young provincial, in fact, until he has finished, as a separate entity, his sight-seeing, does not become even a potential Londoner. He has to exhaust that as he will have to exhaust the personalities, the localities, that for the time being will make up his 'world'. He must have had squeezed swiftly into him all the impressions that the London child has slowly made his own. He must have asked all the ways that are to carry him to and from his daily work; he must be able to find instinctively his own front-door, his own key-hole, his own string that in a noisome cellar pulls the latch, or his own bundle of rags in the corner of a railway arch. Daily details will have merged, as it were, into his bodily functions, and will have ceased to distract his attention. He will have got over the habit of relying, in these things, upon personal contacts. He will have acquired an alertness of eye that will save him from asking his way. On his 'Underground'* he will glance at a board rather than inquire of a porter; on bus-routes he will catch instinctively, on the

advancing and shapeless mass of colour and trade announce-
ments, the small names of taverns, of Crosses,* of what were
once outlying hamlets; he will have in his mind a rough sketch
map of that plot of London that by right of living in he will
make his own. Then he will be the Londoner, and to the measure
of the light vouchsafed will know his London. Yet, to the great
majority of Londoners whose residence is not an *arrière boutique** London will remain a matter of a central highway, a
central tunnel or a central conduit, more or less long; a daily
route whose two extremities are a more or less permanent
sleeping place, and a more or less permanent workshop – a
thing, figured on a map, like the bolas of certain South Ameri-
cans, a long cord with balls at the extremities. At the one there
will gradually congregate the parts of a home, at the other, the
more or less familiar, more or less hypnotising, more or less
congenial, surroundings of his daily work. It will be a matter of
a daily life passing unnoticed.

3

London itself will become the merest abstraction. He will not
moralise upon London. Occasionally a periodical will inform
him with notes of exclamation, that London is a very remarkable
thing. He will read, 'London more than all else in the scenery of
England gives food for thought; this for awe and wonder, not
for boasting, is unique' – and he will acquiesce. Nevertheless
awe and wonder are the last things he will feel.

London, in fact, is so essentially a background, a matter so
much more of masses than of individuals, so much more, as it
were, a very immense symphony-orchestra than a quartette
party with any leader not negligible, that its essential harmony
is not to be caught by any human ear. It can only be treated as
a ground bass, a drone, on top of which one pipes one's own
small individual melody. A human aggregation, it leaves discern-
ible so very little of the human that it is almost as essentially a
natural product as any great stretch of alluvial soil. – Your
marshy delta was brought down in the course of a thousand
years or so. Raindrops, born a long way up in the hills, united
to run through fissures in the earth, through soil-drains, through
runnels in the moss of woods, through channels in the clay of

sodden fields, each drop bearing infinitesimal grains of what, towards the sea at the end, becomes alluvial soil – each drop quarried, each drop carried, each drop endured for its moment, and then went hence and was no more seen. It left the grain of loam it had carried. So precisely out of the clouds of the nations, drops have been born. It is that oblivion, that 'being no more seen', that is, in matters human, the note of London. It never misses, it never can miss anyone. It loves nobody, it needs nobody; it tolerates all the types of mankind. It has palaces for the great of the earth, it has crannies for all the earth's vermin. Palace and cranny, vacated for a moment, find new tenants as equably as the hole one makes in a stream – for, as a critic, London is wonderfully open-minded.

On successive days it will welcome its king going to be crowned, its general who has given it a province, its enemies who have fought against it for years, its potentate guest from Teheran – it will welcome each with identically rapturous cheers. This is not so much because of a fickle-mindedness as because since it is so vast it has audiences for all players. It forgets very soon, because it knows so well that, in the scale of things, any human achievement bulks very small.

It cherishes less than any other town the memory of its mighty dead. Its message for humanity is that it is the business of man to keep all on going, not to climb on to pinnacles. Its street names are those of ground-landlords; its commemorative tablets, on house fronts, are no more to be read than any epitaphs in any churchyards. It is one gigantic pantheon of the dead level of democracy; and, in its essentials it is a home neither for the living nor the dead.

If in its tolerance it finds a place for all eccentricities of physiognomy, of costume, of cult, it does so because it crushes out and floods over the significance of those eccentricities. It, as it were, lifts an eyelid and turns a hair neither for the blue silk gown of an Asiatic, the white robes of a Moor, the kilts of a Highlander, nor the silk hat, inscribed in gold letters with a prophecy of retribution or salvation, of a religious enthusiast. In its innumerable passages and crannies it swallows up Mormon and Mussulman,* Benedictine and Agapemonite,* Jew and Malay, Russian and Neapolitan. It assimilates and slowly digests them, converting them, with the most potent of all juices, into the singular and inevitable product that is the Londoner – that is, in fact, the Modern. Its spirit, extraordinary and unfathom-able – because it is given to no man to understand the spirit of his own age – spreads, like sepia in water, a tinge of its own over all the world. Its extraordinary and miasmic dialect – the dialect of South Essex – is tinging all the local speeches of England. Deep in the New Forest you will find red brick houses trying to look like London villas; deep in the swamps of coastal Africa you will find lay white men trying to remain Londoners, and religious white men trying to turn negroes into suburban chapel worshippers.

London is the world town, not because of its vastness; it is vast because of its assimilative powers, because it destroys all race characteristics, insensibly and, as it were, anaesthetically. A Polish Jew changes into an English Hebrew and then into a Londoner without any legislative enactments, without knowing anything about it. You may watch, say, a Berlin Junker,* arrogant, provincial, unlicked, unbearable to any other German, execrable to anyone not a German, turning after a year or two into a presentable and only just not typical Londoner; subdued, quiet in the matters of collars, ties, coat, voice and backbone, and naturally extracting a 'sir' from a policeman. London will do all this imperceptibly. And, in externals, that is the high-water mark of achievement of the Modern Spirit.

4

Immense without being immediately impressive, tolerant with-out any permanent preferences, attracting unceasingly specimens of the best of all earthly things without being susceptible of any perceptible improvement, London, perhaps because of its utter lack of unity, of plan, of the art of feeling, is the final expression of the Present Stage. It owes its being to no one race, to no two, to no three. It is, as it were, the meeting place of all Occidentals and of such of the Easterns as can come, however remotely, into touch with the Western spirit. Essentially unmusical, in it may be found, as it were 'on show', the best of all music. And it has at odd moments 'on show' the best products of the cook, of the painter, of the flower-gardener, of the engineer, of the religious and of the scientists. It does without any architecture, because in essentials it is an assembly of tents beside a river, a perennial

Nijni Novgorod* bazaar, a permanent world's fair. It is a place
in which one exists in order to gain the means of living out of
it; an epitome, an abstract of the Christian's world, which he
inhabits only to prepare himself for one more bright if less
glamorous. Perhaps, for times to come, some individual of
today, striking the imagination of posterity, may catch and
preserve an entirely individual representation of the London of
today. We have our individual presentations of so many vanished Londons. We have the town of a riverside, with steep,
serrated warehouse-like wharf-dwellings, dominated by a great
Gothic cathedral.* Through its streets wind improbably gigantic
processions of impossibly large mediaeval horsemen. We have a
Tudor London merging into the early Jacobean of the dramatists
– a small, provincial-minded, crooked-streeted, gabled town,
walled, circumscribed, still set in fields whose hedges public-
minded citizens of the train-bands delighted to break down. We
have the two Londons of the diarists* – a London still of
crooked streets, of a Gothic cathedral, with an essential stench,
a glow of torches round house-ends with red crosses on low
doors, a rumble of plague-carts. Then a London rising out of
ashes, with streets, heaven knows, crooked enough, but having
lost its cathedral and its gabled houses. So, perhaps, for the
London of our day.

Some Clerk of the Admiralty is, without doubt, keeping, like
Pepys, his diary; some journalist, like Defoe,* is writing fraudu-
lent memoirs; some caricaturist now before us, some novelist
too much or too little advertised today, will succeed in persuad-
ing posterity that his London is the London that we live in but
assuredly don't know.

We may take that to be certain. Yet it is not so certain that
his London will be as near the real thing as were, in their days,
those of Pepys, of Hogarth, or even of Albert Smith.* One may
hazard that without chanting jeremiads to the art of today. But
we may set it down that Pepys going out from Dover to welcome
Charles II, had somewhere at the back of his head an image of
his London – of a town of a few strongly marked features, of a
certain characteristic outline, of jagged roofs, or over-hanging
upper storeys, of a river that was a highway for ever clamorous
with the cry of 'Oars'.

So, too, had Hogarth when at Calais. Dickens,* posting as
the Uncommercial Traveller towards France over Denmark Hill,

may almost have had an impression of a complete and comparatively circumscribed London. But so many things – as obvious as the enormously increased size, as secondary as the change in our habits of locomotion – militate against our nowadays having an impression, a remembered bird's-eye-view of London as a whole.

The Londoner bites off from his town a piece large enough for his own chewing. We have no symbol of London comparable to the Lutetia* of Paris; none to set beside the figure on the reverse of our copper coins.* It is comparatively easy to have in the mind the idea of a certain green island familiar in its backward tilt towards the shores of Europe, familiar in its rugged outline, in its setting of silver sea. We may think of it as a bit of coloured marble-facing broken from a palace wall, with counties mottled in green, counties in pink, counties in buff, in blue, in yellow. We may think of it embossed in relief out of a robin's-egg blue sea, with the misty white cliffs of Kent, the slate and marble of Devon, the serpentine of Cornwall, or the half-submerged rafts of the outer Hebrides forming the edges.

It is, in fact, comparatively easy to evoke a picture of England as a whole, still easier, perhaps, to think of this world as a green orange revolving round a candle, or as the pink and blue of a Mercator's projection.* One may sail easily round England, or circumnavigate the globe. But not the most enthusiastic geographer – one must of course qualify these generalisations with an 'as a rule' – ever memorised a map of London. Certainly no one ever walks round it. For England is a small island, the world is infinitesimal amongst the planets. But London is illimitable.

5

A brilliant, wind-swept, sunny day, with the fountains like hay-cocks* of prismatic glitter in the shadow of Nelson's Column, with the paving stones almost opalescent, with colour everywhere, the green of the orange trees in tubs along the façade of the National Gallery, the vivid blue of the paper used by flower-sellers to wrap poet's narcissi, the glint of straws blown from horses' feeds, the shimmer of wheel-marks on the wood pavement, the shine of bits of harness, the blaze of gold lettering along the house fronts, the slight quiver of the nerves after a momentarily dangerous crossing accentuating the perception – is that 'London'? Does that rise up in your Londoner's mind's eye, when, in the Boulevard Haussman, or on the Pyramids,* he thinks of his own places?

Or is it the chaotic crowd, like that of baggage wagons huddled together after a great defeat, blocked in the narrow ways of the City, an apparently indissoluble muddle of gray wheel traffic, of hooded carts, of buses drawing out of line, of sticky mud, with a pallid church wavering into invisibility towards the steeple in the weeping sky, of grimy upper windows through which appear white faces seen from one's level on a bus-top, of half the street up, of the monstrous figure of a horse 'down' – and surely there is no more monstrous apparition than that of a horse down in the sticky streets with its frantic struggles, the glancing off of its hoofs, the roll of eyes, the sudden apparition of great teeth, and then its lying still – is this, with its black knot of faces leaning a little over the kerbstone, with its suggestion of the seashore in the unconcerned, tarpaulin-shrouded figure of the traffic policeman – is this again 'London', the London we see from a distance?

Or do we see it in the glare of kerosene lamps, the diffused blaze of shop fronts, the slowly moving faces revealed for a moment, then as it were, washed out, of the serried, marketing crowds. They will be carrying string bags, carrying paper parcels, carrying unwrapped green stuff, treading on layers of handbills, treading on the white scrolls of orange peels, on small heaps of muddy sawdust, standing in shawled groups round the glare of red joints in butchers' shops, standing in black groups round the carts of nostrum sellers, round the carts of dutch auctioneers; with ears deafened by the cries of vendors of all things meet for a Saturday night, by the incessant whistle of trams looming at a snail's pace through the massed humanity; by the incessant, as if vindictively anvil-like, peals of notes of barrel organs. In a patch of shadow left in a vacant space, you will hardly make out the figure of a forlorn man standing still. With a pendent placard on his chest, announcing one of the ills of the flesh, he offers for sale things that you would think nobody could stop to buy, or indistinguishable quavers of melody that nobody could stay to hear. Is this again the London that comes to one at a distance?

For, almost assuredly, it will be some minute detail of the

whole, we seeing things with the eye of a bird that is close to the ground. And with the eye of a bird seeking for minute fragments of seed, minute insects, tiny parasites, we also look for things that to us are the constituents of our mental or visual pabula.* The tendency of 'carriage folk' must be to think of the Saturday night market as nothing but the swinging doors of public-houses and of pawnshops, as nothing but the architectural arrangements of translucent gin bottles in pale shop windows. The marketer has his tendency to regard those he sees in carriages as insolent servants conducting people who 'are no better than they should be'. The essential Bohemian must think of those whose sign visual is the aligned brass knockers of suburban streets, as sluggish-minded and intolerable. Thus, humanity not caring to think about what it does not like, the villa resident away from London will see a vision of 'Parks' and 'Gardens', surrounded by uninteresting or repulsive districts of small houses; the working man thinks of High Streets, of small streets, of tenement blocks, set down on the fringes of villadom.

The limits of the classes are not of course so crudely definite but that there is an infinity of individual variants. There are the crowds of philanthropists who make swallow flights into slums, the mechanics who dream of their own carriages. There is room for millennialists who strive to create Garden Cities,* for socialist prophets who read in the skies signs of an approaching Armageddon* after which all men shall be alike in tastes as in habituation. But in the bulk the Londoner is anything rather than tolerant of a class not his own; the unfamilar is almost inevitably the iniquitous.

We may, among the October partridges, have a sudden vision of a slinking, horribly suggestive pair of figures. We saw them as we walked gaily home from the very best ball of last season, in the pale delicate stillness of dawn, at the mouth of a black court, under the unclean light of a street lamp held out from a dirty wall by a bracket, as if an arm were holding a torch to comment on the blackness of the inwards of this earth. And those figures, slinking back into those shadows, may among the crisp stubble suddenly rise up and stand for London.

Or one may as a child, have crept out of a slum on a summer night, have climbed some area railings in a long street all railings, to peep in at a room where the delicate, tender light of candles shimmering on silver, on the shining shoulders of

women, on the shining linen of men, contended with the
delicate, tender light of the London sunset. And that picture
may rise up for one in the shadows of a black Kentish barn,
where in the hopping season* straw-thatched hurdles pen off
the darkness, and the air is heavy with the odour of hops, of
rags, of humanity. But, essentially, the London that from afar
the Londoner sees is his own parish, and his own parish is the
part he knew in his youth, the human stratum from which he
started. A man may have passed right across London in his life;
he may have dropped as it were from ledge to ledge; he may
have been born in Mayfair to fall in his traces, a sodden beast,
outside a public-house of the Tower Hamlets. Or he may have
been born in the fifth of a room in a Whitechapel ghetto, to die
in a palace of Park Lane. Yet assuredly the London of the one
will be, not the purlieus of Bankruptcy Buildings, not the shabby
lodgings, not the dismal blind-yard in which sandwich-boards
are given out, not any of the intermediate stages, but the West
of his youth. He will die thinking himself a gentleman. And –
one may hazard the induction – the standard by which the other
will appraise the world-centre he has conquered will be the
auction for the right to open the tabernacle in the synagogue,*
the inscriptions in the kosher shops, the grating of the *lingua-
hebraica*, the casting of sins at the feast of the New Year into
the tidal waters off the parapet of Custom House Wharf, the
feather of the Day of Purification, that were his familiars when
a young lad. The middle stages of neither will have counted as,
in middle life, the mind lost its impressionability.

Besides which, to see London steadily and see it whole, a man
must have certain qualities of temperament so exhaustive as to
preclude, on the face of it, the faculties which go to the making
– or the marring – of great fortunes. He must, it is true, have his
'opportunities'. But before all things he must have an
impressionability and an impersonality, a single-mindedness to
see, and a power of arranging his illustrations cold-bloodedly,
an unemotional mind and a great sympathy, a life-long engross-
ment in his 'subject', and an immense knowledge, for purposes
of comparison, of other cities. He must have an avidity and a
sobriety of intellect, an untirable physique and a delicately
tempered mind. These things are antitheses.

An intelligent foreigner running through a town of strongly
marked features may carry away a definite impression of its

character and its life, although he will inevitably go astray in point of statistics, of etiquette, or local history. But of London no foreignness, which implies an openness to impressions – and no clear intelligence, can, in the lump, make much.

A Paris journalist lamented the gross indecency of London in the matter of the nude. He had taken his first walk in London with a lady friend, near the Serpentine, during the hours when bathing is permitted. An Italian royal Marchioness sighed because there were no birds in England. She had, on the occasion of an international function, spent three November days as a royal guest in Buckingham Palace. A Portuguese diplomatist never travelled in England save armed to the teeth. On his first journey from Dover to London he had been rather roughly handled by card sharpers. An American commercial magnate speaks of London as the most radiant and friendly place, because his first impression was at a private house, of the white cap and apron, pink cheeks, low voice, and welcoming smiles of a housemaid at the door. I have never been able to persuade a Jesuit Father, a friend of my own, to visit London, because of Bill Sikes and Fagin's academy* for thieves.

Away from his town, with no picture of his own in his mind, that is what the Londoner will be brought up against – a Cimmerian* district where, in a gloom so dense that no bird can see to carry straws to its nest, naked men run pallidly in and out of crowds of card-sharpers, lightened here and there by house-maids, shadowed always by starvation, drink, crime, and the drippings of tallow candles that are to be seen in plates after Cruikshank.* He won't, if he has any contact with foreigners, ever get away from it.

Seated at a continental card-table with a 'quite nice', capped and mittened, smiling old lady, he will find the game suddenly suspended. The courteous and restrained smile with which a good Catholic asks a heretic about the outrageous practises of his sect, will beam upon the old lady's face. She will say that she cannot understand how anyone so obviously humane and sympathetic as the particular Londoner before her, can bear to walk the streets of London town, where, at all moments and on all sides, people suddenly drop dead of starvation. She will resume her deal.

Confronted with this particular 'View of London' your Londoner can only gasp. He will realise that his amiable hostess has been reading, in her local paper, a quotation from his Registrar General's returns. And, for purposes of refutation, the trouble is that he knows nothing about the figures. He does not feel assured whether, according to the Return, 75, 750, or 7,500 people died of starvation during the past year. He does not know whether 'cases of death from exposure accelerated by want' are included. He has a hazy notion that no one in London need die of starvation, seeing that there are workhouses. But as a rule he knows nothing of the workings of Poor Law Relief.* He knows so little of his London.

He may even, as a result, have added to his particular picture of the place, the dim and disturbing image of a lank-haired, hollow cheeked, glaring eyed, pale woman, – a Spectre of Starvation with, in the bulge of an old shawl, the suggestion of a naked, frozen baby. He will not have seen them in the Kensington-plus-Cornhill that is his London. But an intangible cloud-like population of white-faced misery, may come suddenly to disturb his ideas of Hoxton or Highgate, of Shoreditch or of Canning Town. Or the comparatively contented mechanician is suddenly confronted with his continental confrère's picture of the luxury, the profusion, the lust, the wantonness, of a foreign view of Hyde Park. In front of the dark eyes, the flashing teeth, the blue blouse, he will grow uncomfortably uncertain whether, outside his own Walthamstow of small pleasant houses, all the valley of the Thames is not Sodom and Gomorrah.* Once away from the few facts that he can, as it were, catch hold of with his hands, he knows, your Londoner, so appallingly little of his London. It isn't his business; he has his own affairs. In the gigantic tool-basket of a place he can find pretty well whatever he needs. He will be surprised if others cannot.

6

London is a great, slip-shod, easy-going, good-humoured magnet; those it attracts are much of a muchness with itself. They have not any Corporate spirit in particular. And the Londoner when talked to by inhabitants of other considerable towns is apt to be violently confronted with what he hasn't. It is not only that in Essen or Düsseldorf he will learn that he has no factories each employing sixteen skilled chemists continually analysing slag-heaps for by-products; that he has not any secondary schools worth the mention; that his workmen are not efficiently organised, or that his capitalists do not squeeze the last drop of blood out of their men. But nearer home he will learn more severe lessons.

Let him go to one of the larger towns well outside his Home Counties, and he will have it forced in on him that he has no municipal buildings costing wellnigh a million, that he has no ship-canals, that his atmosphere has not half the corrosive properties that it should have to betoken the last word of wealth, of progress, and of commercial energy. He will be told that he has nothing worth having, and that he is infinitely too proud of what he has. Yet as a rule the accusation is unkind. However proud the Londoner may be of his personality, of his wife, of his wine, or of the poultry run in his back garden, the last thing he would think of being proud of is London. His most considerable exhibition of pride will appear in his mild disgust, if he is mistaken for a provincial. He is singularly useless as a Defender of the city's fame. He will know of a Mansion House,* but he will probably not know whether it is a municipal place of business or merely the residence of a chief magistrate; he will have a vague idea that something goes on at Spring Gardens.* He would not, on the other hand, be certain whether London contained a University, or, tucked away in some corner, a ship canal. He goes through life with the comforting thought that somewhere there are people one might ask, or very good postal directories. In Rhenish-Westphalia he will be assured that London is already as deserted as Bruges. His eyes will have told him that that is not the case today. But, set there in the hideous heart of the German competition he so much dreads, confronted by the blackened landscape, by miles of gray slag mounds, by horizons obscured with rusty cinder heaps, by heaps of sand, by heaps of rust, by clouds of green, of red, of purple, or of black smoke, by dirt of the foulest and labour of the obviously grimmest, he will not be certain of the day-after-tomorrow of London. He will almost certainly not know that, in the marshes round Purfleet, he has factories larger, more modern, better capitalised, more solvent, and a landscape more blackened and more grim.

The Westphalian will say: 'Oh yes, it is all over', and before the Londoner's mental picture of his little bit of the city and suburbs there will rise up a view of the stained and deserted

façades of a London like Bruges, with swarms of pauper children
tumbling over the doorsteps, and an old gray horse cropping the
grass between the flagstones of Threadneedle Street. He will not
in the least know what reserves of wealth or of energy his
London may have.

7

Above all his London, his intimate London, will be the little bits
of it that witnessed the great moments, the poignant moods of
his life; it will be what happened to be the backgrounds of his
more intense emotions.

Certain corners of streets, certain angles of buildings, the
spray of dishevelled plane-trees, certain cloud-forms, gusts of
white smoke, odours, familiar sounds – these, in their remembrance will wring his heart. He will have noticed them, or hardly
noticed them, glancing aside in his moments of terror, of
perplexity, of passion, of grief. And the remembrance of them,
a long way away, will bring up again, tempered by the glamour
of memory, by the romance of old days, the reflection of those
griefs, of those terrors, of those old piteousnesses.

For London is before all things an incomparable background;
it is always in the right note, it is never out of tone. A man may
look down out of dim windows upon the slaty, black, wet
misery of a squalid street, upon a solitary flickering lamp that
wavers a sooty light upon a solitary, hurrying passer's umbrella.
He may have received a moment before the first embrace of a
woman, or a moment before his doctor may have told him that
he is not very long for this world. He will stand looking down;
and a sudden consonance with his mood, of overwhelming and
hardly comprehensible joy, of overwhelming and hardly fath-
omable pain, a sudden significance will be there in the black wet
street, in the long wavering reflections on the gleaming paving-
stones, in the engrossed hurry of the passer-by. It will become,
intimately and rightly, the appropriate background for a beginning of, or for a farewell from life – for the glow of a commenced
love or for the dull pain of a malady ending only in death. It is
that, more than anything, that London has ready for every man.

It can provide a background for everything. With the sympathy of the weeping heavens, or the irony of other men's

unconcern, it remains always a background; it never obtrudes. A man may be so soothingly alone – with his joys as with his griefs.

We may hurry across the great stretches and folds of a park, with a glamorous smirched sunset, curling clouds over the distant houses, wisps of mist becoming palpably blue against thorn trees and the call of a closing space and of a closing in day, indescribably mournful and distant. We may hurry to our triumph of love, to our bankruptcy, to our end or our beginning of the world. Or we may be driven behind a slipping, frightened horse through gray empty streets, among whirls of small hard snowflakes, to a house where there are the titter and bustle of a wedding, or where on the stairs there are the heavy footfalls and muffled breathings of men carrying down the coffin of our best friend in the world. The background for either mood will be the right one. It is these things that come back to us at a distance and in odd ways. I have known a man, dying a long way from London, sigh queerly for a sight of the gush of smoke that, on a platform of the Underground, one may see, escaping in great woolly clots up a circular opening, by a grimy, rusted iron shield, into the dim upper light. He wanted to see it again as others have wished to see once more the Bay of Naples, the olive groves of Catania. Another wanted – how very much he wanted! – to see once more the sort of carpet of pigeons on the gravel in front of a certain Museum steps; the odd top-hatted unpresentable figure of a battered man, holding a paper of bun crumbs, with pigeons on his shoulders, on his hands, crowding in between his feet and fluttering like an aureole of wings round his head.

London is a thing of these 'bits'. It is seldom that one sees at one time as much of it as one may always see of any country town. It has nothing, it never had anything, worth talking of as a spectacular expression of humanity, of that incongruous jumble of races that is in England. It has no Acropolis, no Forum Romanum, no Champs Elysées; it has not so much as a Capitol or a Nevski Prospekt. The tombs of its Kings, its Valhalla,* its Senate, are, relatively to London nowhere in particular. Viewed from a distance it is a cloud on the horizon. From the dark, further side of the Surrey hills at night, above the inky sky line of heather, of pine tops, of elms, one may see on the sky a brooding and sinister glow. That is London – manifesting itself on the clouds.

CHAPTER 2

Roads into London

Is it where the glow on the sky is no longer seen that 'the country' ends and the influence of London begins? I can scarcely tell even where that is. I have heard that it can be seen from near Colchester; from near Maidstone I have seen it myself. But these 'shays'* of the larger towns can be caught from very far: I have distinguished that of such a town as Folkestone from nearly thirty miles away.

Speaking a little arbitrarily, we may say that there are three Londons. There is the psychological London, where the London spirit is the note of life, there is the Administrative County, and there is the London of natural causes, the assembly of houses in the basin of the lower Thames.

To where then do the spheres of influence of these three Londons reach out? Frankly, I do not know, and I have asked myself the question many times. The Administrative County* includes so little of psychological London. Chislehurst, for instance, psychologically considered, is London; so, in their own ways, are Brighton, Hastings, Southend-on-Sea, parts of the Riviera, and half of the Essex flats.*

Highbury, I should say, is London, because the greater part of its inhabitants get their 'supplies' from The Stores, and go for their intellectual stimulants to a place in Oxford Street. Thus the stores and the circulating library make London extend to Jubbulpore and to the married officers' bungalows on the Irawaddy. I heard the other day from an administrator of those parts. He was living in ruined temples, but his clothes, his boots, his whips, his tinned meats, his sauces, his mustard and his wines came from the one institution; he was astonishingly 'well up' in the books of the year, better certainly than most London reviewers, because of the other. He had, too, a phonograph, which supplied him with piano music from St James's Hall and the latest songs of the empire. These ruined temples where he camped for the night became little pieces of London; and we have lately had a Viceroy of India lamenting that Tottenham Court Road has stretched into the zenanas* of the native states.

Yet in many places within the Administrative County the tendency is all towards 'localising', or towards remaining separate centres. In Hampstead, for instance, the older residents buy most things of the local tradesmen, and newer families imitate them for sentimental or for social reasons. In poorer neighbourhoods this is much more the case. Old places of entertainment, like the Horns Assembly Rooms, flourish, and large theatres spring up along the tram-lines. I think there are no local daily papers, though in the dark heart of the docks knots of men stand round blank walls. On these journalists, having the same relation to those of Fleet Street as the pavement artist has to Academicians, chalk in capital letters details of the last murders, divorces, and wrecks. And the people of the poorer suburbs do their shopping in their own High Streets. Where great local emporia have not crushed out altogether the 'local tradesman', shoppers with string bags still nod at the greengrocer and the oilman when passing or when making their purchases.

One cannot, therefore, limit psychological London by the glow on its sky, to the sphere of influence of the stores, or to the Administrative County.

Administrative London, on the other hand, ignores alike the psychological and the natural. It administers in a sensible rule of thumb way South Kensington and Bermondsey, the sewers of slums and great expanses of green land. The natural features of London are obscured, but they underlie the others patiently. They are the hills that made possible the basin of the Thames, the oldest of all the roads into London; they are the old marshes and flat lands on which it was so easy to build. They show still a little in open hilly spaces of the outlying ring, in odd bits of forest here and there, in level commons, like those near Clapham, where there are still many ponds. No doubt, in the ultimate fullness of time, these hills, forests, and marshes will resume their sway.

But nowadays we may say that London begins where tree trunks commence to be black, otherwise there is very little to distinguish Regent's Park from Penshurst, or Wimbledon from Norwich. This tree-trunk boundary is, however, defective enough; in many parts of Epping the wood is so dense that boughs and the boulders are as green, as brown, as mossy or as lichened as at Fontainebleau. The prevailing winds being from the south and from the westwards, again, the zone of blackened trunks extends further than is fair towards the north and the east. But judged by this standard, London, as far as I have been able to observe, is bounded by a line drawn from Leigh, in Essex, halfway through the Epping Forest, to the north of Hendon, to the west of Brentford, the southwest of Barnes, well to the south of Sydenham, well to the east of Bromley, and so up to Leigh again. Other observers will, no doubt, find this tree-trunk limitation a little faulty; but it takes in at least nearly all the looser elements of the sphere of London influence. And, as the invariable and bewildering exception to this, as to all rules, it may as well be set down that the most 'Londony' of all London trees has a bark that is never uniformly black. The plane tree grows best of all in London, because it sheds its bark continually; getting rid of its soot it clears the pores of its skin and flourishes, if I may be allowed an image that appears frivolous but that is sober enough, a perpetual emblem to the city of the morning tub. In the suburbs the plane yields first place to the flowering almond, in the parks to the thorn, but it is the tree of intimate London.

Elms, however, are the trees most noticeable on the roads into London, and their trunks blacken perhaps soonest of all. Nine Elms, Barn Elms,* and how many other 'Elms'? greet us on the run into town; and the feathery outlines of how many of these trees close the vistas of those new suburban streets that are for ever drilling little pathways into the ancient 'estates' of the home counties? To return again to the oldest of all roads into London, elms standing on rising ground have formed familiar landmarks for twenty centuries before there were beacons, lighthouses, buoys, or pilots on the river.

For the 'question' of London, seen from one point of view, resolves itself into that one of highways; and the very origin of London, the first cause of its existence, is that waterway. Nowadays we have discovered, as if in the night, a new secret of rapid communication: with that, as with every previous modification of the kind, the face of London bids fair to change unrecognisably. Whilst the pen is actually on my paper London is spreading itself from Kew towards Hounslow, towards Richmond, and towards Kingston, and on its other bounds towards how many other outlying places? The electric tram* is doing all this.

To come into a city by means of one of these new, swift carriages, to come from any distance, say by a motor car, is to fly too fast for any easy recognition of the gradual changes from country to town. There are hedgerows, church towers moving rapidly as if drawn along among clumps of trees, on the horizon; then come brickfields, inn signs, more signboards, a roadside house, bits of paper on the footpath, then a bus, dust whitening hedges, whitening them more, a villa, half a dozen villas, then new shops set one into another without a break, a swift glimpse of a great plain of roofs, gray and without visible limits, a long way below; a swift drop down a slope – a drop that one feels more internally than through the eyes – and one is dodging the close traffic, slowing down, slipping past a dray, boring a hansom in towards the pavement, and it is all over.

We stepped into the thing in our own farmyard; we seem to come to ourselves only in the middle of the familiar things of town, in the light filtering down between the tall buildings, before our own white doorstep, and the outstretched hand, pale in the palm, brown in the fingers, of an urchin who has, or has not, saved the lady's dress from touching the wheel, is before us. We have not been able to differentiate Mill Hill from the Welsh Harp* district; Brentford was Chiswick and the Goldhawk Road before one had left the upper river; the Old Kent Road became the Borough High Street after we were hardly out of Maidstone.

It is not so much that the speed is very great, there is always the statutory limit, a sort of nightmare; but the motorist is too low down as a rule, the air presses against the eyes and half closes them; he has a tendency to look forward along the road, to see more of vehicles and of pedestrians than of the actual country or the regiments of buildings. He grows a little aloof, a little out of sympathy; he becomes more intent about keeping a whole skin on himself and on his car than about the outer world.

This is doubtless no more than a matter of time, of 'getting used to it', or of thinking of distances, as it were, in terms of the motor car. One has been accustomed to drive on a bus from Kensington to Piccadilly Circus in the half hour. One has seen the tall flats by Sloane Street for some minutes, Apsley House* for some more minutes, and one was used to look down on the Green Park from a certain angle for a certain space of leisurely transit. These things have their familiar aspects.

They grow unfamiliar on the motor car. The motorist is, as I have said, low down, he pulls up before no buildings; narrow streets like the old Kensington High Street present the aspect of tortuous defiles; he dodges in and out as if he were being whirled on a current through the rocky gorge of a river. Hyde Park Corner opens out suddenly like the flat reach below Coblentz on the Rhine. But we shall grow used to that, too.

What the automobile is to the comfortable classes the electric tram is becoming to the poorer. It is a means of getting into town. It does not, however, produce the same psychological effects. For one thing, the speed is not so great, and you have not the least anxiety as to what it may choose to run into; if you want to see things you are at a greater height, your range of sight is much longer. You may pick out upon the pavement any strange object; a tall negro with a blue birds-eye handkerchief round his head, eating, with the motions of a large ape, winkles out of a blue paper bag – or a girl with extremely brilliant red hair. You pick them out from a distance and watch them for a minute or two; you may look down at passing, you may look round. The other day I saw from the top of an electric tram, very far away, above the converging lines in the perspective of a broad highway of new shops, a steam crane at work high in the air on an upper storey. The thin arm stretched out above the street, spidery and black against a mistiness that was half sky, half haze; at the end of a long chain there hung diagonally some baulks of wood, turning slowly in mid-air. They were rising imperceptibly, we approaching imperceptibly. A puff of smoke shot out, writhed very white, melted and vanished between the housefronts. We glided up to and past it. Looking back I could see down the reverse of the long perspective the baulks of timber turning a little closer to the side of the building, the thin extended arm of the crane a little more foreshortened against the haze. Then the outlines grew tremulous, it all vanished with a touch of that pathos like a hunger that attaches to all things of which we see the beginnings or the middle courses without knowing the ends. It was impressive enough – the modern spirit expressing itself in terms not of men but of forces, we gliding by, the timbers swinging up, without any visible human action in either motion. No doubt men were at work in the engine-belly of the crane, just as others were very far away among the dynamos that kept us moving. But they were sweating invisible. That, too, is the Modern Spirit: great organisations run by men as impersonal as the atoms of our own frames, noiseless, and to all appearances infallible.

At night, too, when the broad flat streets out in the suburbs are deserted, these electric trams appear romantic and a little wonderful. Gongs sound at their approach rather plaintively, headlights blaze out upon the black night, the lights within are a tall, mellow flood, a reflection is cast, dim and flying, upon old black houses behind trees and upon the large, blank windows of the tall pink and terracotta shops that face them. The great rectangular blaze glides along with a heavy, impersonal groan of sound that is like a new form of silence, the figure of the mechanician in front has a backward rake like that of a man in the bows of a boat; as it passes there is the gleam of a long row of pink faces in the heart of the light. And all these things, the clang of the gongs, the rumble growing and dying away, the strong lights, the momentary and half revealed details of the darkened buildings, the thought of all these people going out a long way to sleep in the blacker darkness, have about them something touching and romantic, something 'characteristic' and foreign.

Of the older methods of communication I suppose the bicycle to come next, but I have always found entering London in this way to be tedious and dispiriting. You have to attend to yourself even more particularly than when you are in a motor-car; you have only half a horizon – the half that is in front of you. You are nearer the dust when there is dust, or nearer the mud. Transition from country to town becomes rather wearisome; you think a good deal in miles. London manifests itself slowly with high-banked and gravelled footpaths, with those same blackened tree trunks, in a certain coarseness of the grass, in houses of call that you feel uninclined to call at. Dogcarts and governess cars begin to look a little out of place, indefinably, you don't know why. And suddenly you meet a bus.

I don't know whether it is to me alone that a bus running between hedgerows seems forlorn and incongruous. They 'link up' all sorts of outlying villages – Mitcham with Tooting, all sorts of hamlets with Kingston-on-Thames, Islington with I don't quite know where. There is a network of what are called bus-routes all over England, but these are mostly carrier's carts. Some have tarpaulin hoods and go at a walk, others look like the station omnibuses of country hotels. Their existence is largely unsuspected, yet it is possible to go from Lewes to York by changing from link to link in market towns, or from Canterbury to Sydenham.

But the just-outside-London bus carries no parcels. It is, as a rule, bright green, and has a brilliant orange knifeboard* atop. It goes at a good pace, and it is the sign that you have reached the sphere of influence of the very outer suburbs. I at least have never entered London by road without meeting or passing one of them.

They are due to the enterprise of large job masters near the great tram and London omnibus termini; they are the signs of London's reaching out its arms still further; they are really the pioneers. In older days they started from Whitehall, from the Bank,* from the Borough, and were called Short Stages. As real London spreads they cease to pay; they travel farther afield, and their place is taken by our municipal services or by those of the larger trusts.

It is a long time since I have come into London on foot, so long that I have forgotten what it feels like. Indeed, I fancy that the proceeding is no longer modern, and is in consequence illegitimate to my purpose. Some tramps do it still, I suppose, and the gipsies who walk beside basket caravans. These, we may say, are as much the country stretching into the suburbs as the buses are the town stretching out. It is not very usual to meet them in inner London, though I have seen two or three at a time, with their chimneys smoking, entangled in the centre of the Piccadilly buses themselves. They were crossing London thus directly in order to get as soon as possible from some horse fair in Berkshire to another in North Kent – Rochester pleasure fair, I think, because it was towards the end of May. But except when there is some such reason for haste, these caravans rarely cross London. They circle it by the roads just inside the suburbs. Only yesterday, about six miles from Whitehall, I passed twice the mouth of a dingy and sinister passage of small eighteenth century houses. It was called Angel Court. Fifty years ago it was in the fields, now its entry was between a large modern public house and a large modern pawnshop. I glanced down it, walking outwards;

it was empty, silent and sordid. On my return there were in it four or five dark men with heavy, brass-bound whips, eight or nine dark women, and several children with black or red heads. In four or five of the small new streets that ran at right angles to my road there were caravans covered with basket chairs, osier flower-stands, wicker baskets; women were holding these things up in front of the lace curtains of sitting-room windows.

These people are not mere picturesque survivals; their number increases day by day as poorer men find the hurry of modern life too great; but I cannot claim to have entered London in a pikey's* cart. I fancy, however, that looking at things through the small square of a back window, being at home in the middle of strange things, the sense too of being very aloof from the rest of the world must make one's point of view rather a special one. One would become more or less of a foreign observer.

That attitude, backed up by that sense of being at home, is the worst that one could assume; it kills even tolerance for the habits of others. It is the reason why the days of most rapid travelling are the days of most frequent misunderstandings between the races of mankind. Your foreigner, reaching his London in a Pullman car, has been during his whole journey in an hotel, very much like one of his own hotels, not very much unlike his own home. He stepped into it in St Petersburg an arrogant Tartar or a wily Slav; he steps down from it in the dim light of Charing Cross. He has gone through none of the processes of travel, none of his edges have been rubbed off, he is not necessarily the best type of Russian. He is quite ready to kick a porter and be cursed for it. He dislikes the place he has come to, and records his hasty impressions in letters home that may become so many international causes of misunderstanding.

In the slower days it was different. He was sent abroad because he was the best type of his race, or he came because he was a fine and adventurous spirit. He came from Moscow on sledges, in travelling carriages, on foot, by ship to Hull, overland to London. He had plenty of preparation, plenty of hardship to rub the angles down, and he was very glad to reach his journey's end. He expected to find savages, he found amiable and civilised white men; he reported well of the place he had reached. If an ambassador, he was polished, cosmopolitan, and pleasing; if an adventurer, he was a fine spirit. He had all sorts of tales to tell of escapes, of strange things seen by the way. He became a delightful person; he was full of deference for local customs, because his life or his livelihood depended on his ability to please. (I am thinking of the evidence given at the trial of Count Königsmarck* in London by a crowd of Swedish, Russian, and Bohemian soldiers, stable-boys and hangers on. Or one may evidence Casanova,* who was pleased and pleased himself in London; or you may read in Mr Round's 'Commune of London'* how great a part in the twelfth century foreign merchants, cut off from their own lands, played in exacting from the Angevin kings* the liberty of London herself.)

It was the same with those whom London sent out. The few – the gentlemen and the merchant-adventurers – went, say, to the Spice Islands. The hardships of a long voyage, the great mysteries of seas and skies, chastened what of their souls was insular. They went among strange peoples with minds ready to be delighted. They sought, perhaps, nothing more romantic than pepper, but for their lives' sakes they respected local traditions, and were ready to kneel with their faces to the ground when a Soldan went past. They had left their homes so far behind them.

And this, indeed, is the 'defect of the quality' of rapid travel. The Londoner abroad is no longer sought after, fêted, a messenger of the goodness of his race, as were Congreve, Chesterfield, Gibbon, and, in another way, Richardson.* Nowadays in the flood of him he has become the tweed-suited, long-toothed being of caricatures. The defect of the quality, because the traveller now, like the gipsy, takes his home and his home-spirit so much with him. And the one and the other are apt to find that every man's hand is against him.

Yet if that be the defect, the product of the quality of rapid transit is London itself. France has its Ministry of Roads and Bridges, and that is probably why Paris is not France: we have none, and London is England. It began by London's settling on the best placed highway in Europe, and England is still very much tied to the Thames. But France is little dependent on the Seine. Her excellent roads have in times past acted as the great decentralisers; Paris has been merely the administrative city. In England administration has remained with fair constancy at Westminster, near enough to the centre of the country. Wealth has always come into England by the Thames at London. At any rate in later centuries, the tendency has been for the

Administration to settle near the centres of wealth,[1] and the combined attractions have made the tract of marsh and flat ground in the lower basin of the river the centre of the Arts, of the Industries, of the Recreations and of the moral 'tone', not for England alone but for wider regions of the earth.

The roads into London have always been the crucial matter. They remain both the 'question' and the cause of that question. The first parliament of the twentieth century that might have devoted all its deliberation to the internal affairs of the country opened in 1903. The first question it discussed was that of Housing in London.

The question is not merely topical to the first years of the twentieth century; it has been the sempiternal question, it will remain unsolved until London and the country begin to fall into decay. It is, in fact, the 'old' question, and just as today the alternative to rapid transit is the erecting of tall buildings, so it was in the old days for ever. The story has been the same down to the minute details.

The Thames was for sixteen centuries the great highway of intercommunication within London walls. London streets were mere footways or bridlepaths between house-walls; when Queen Elizabeth went abroad on land she was carried in a litter by her gentlemen; there were on Thames-side 40,000 watermen, till the middle of the seventeenth century. Then suddenly:

> Fulsome madams and new scurvy squires
> Did jolt the streets in pomp at their desires . . .
> Drawn by the pampered jades of Belgia* . . .

---

[1] This tendency was always observable in English history. It became, however, most observable with the eighteenth century. Before then, as in the days of John or during the wars of the Roses, to lose London was not to lose the country. Henry VII indeed held London, but to the end of his reign had practically no administrative power over England at large, and until quite late Henry VIII was powerless, save in the Home Counties. Parliaments, too, were held wherever the Kings might happen to be in force. But already with the Stewarts to lose London was to lose England. It was so with Charles I, and so with James II. And the last chance of the Pretender's vanished with the establishment of the National Debt. The Chevalier could get no adherents in England, largely because the wealthy classes feared that he would repudiate. That in fact was the personal influence of London wealth on the country at large. And from that day forth it has seemed more and more impossible that a parliament should be held anywhere but in London.*

That almost all the streets are choked outright
Whilst watermen want work.

Horse-drawn carriages had been introduced.

The cry is that of Taylor the water poet* and a waterman himself. It was that of the stage coachmen when railways came in, it will be that of the cabmen tomorrow, of railway engineers on the day after. That is the detail.

But until the days of Taylor London had been growing year by year more congested. Originally there had been the Tower, a fortress-village with a walled town of mud huts round it, its roads mere footpaths, its space circumscribed enough. As the town grew more important feudal nobles built palaces on the banks of the stream, crowds vast for their day came on foot or horse from the surrounding country or in ships from outer Europe. The houses of London climbed skywards along the narrow lanes – 'Elizabethan' houses, half-timbered, climbing up to six, eight and ten storeys, the upper ones bulging out and almost touching overhead to gain in the air the space that had to be ceded to foot traffic on the ground. Near the river were these houses of the 'comfortable' classes. These palaces of the kings and the great houses of the nobles crowded the face of the river that their owners might keep their private barges and have their own water gates. The others at the public stairs called 'Oars!' as today we call 'Cab'. Then came 'the pampered jades of Belgia'.

Roads were laid down or made up to suit them, then London spread out and the watermen disappeared or starved. (Taylor died a 'victualler' at Oxford.) The poorer classes began to swarm into such of the tall, 'comfortable' houses as the Fire left, the nobles moved their houses on to the larger roads, the comfortable classes built themselves small houses. The riverside palaces became wharfingers'* buildings, their gardens and water gates became quays. Exactly the same thing has happened with every subsequent improvement in communications.

Ten years ago tall flats for the comfortable and tall dwellings for workmen seemed to have solved the question. The latter are already discredited, the former have always been disliked, and London is once more sending out bee swarms of small houses. We may consider that the thousands and thousands of small brick, slate-roofed cottages on the flats and low hills of south

Essex are the contribution of 'workmen's fares'.* These, though
still growing, are old-fashioned already, so quickly do we move.
The electric tractions are, as it were, spreading layers of the tall
flats in villas over new regions of the south and west. London is
full of traces of these past stages.

You may find an old water gate at the bottom of Buckingham
Street; Somerset House* and Whitehall and Westminster palaces
remain administrative long after kings and protectors have left
the lower river; all over the west central district there are august
Georgian houses with panelled rooms and 'ceilings by Adams',*
inhabited by family upon family of the most entirely poor, or by
firm upon firm, in stages one above another, of solicitors, of
architects, of money lenders, of journalists.

Varying types of houses are buried in all parts of London in a
way that is bewildering and makes classification impossible.
They are like the stratifications of pottery and rubble that lie
under all large cities, Rome and London alike. But it is as if the
layers had been disturbed. It is not necessary to cite such
artificially respected fragments as the mediaeval St John's Gate*
at Clerkenwell, which in any city less prodigal of relics would
be a place of pilgrimage for sightseers, or the old house in
Holborn. These are not factors in the life of modern London.

But on certain of the great roads into Town you will see the
queerest jumble of old terraces, shadowed by old trees, grimed
by the soot of generations long dead, jostled by the newest of
shops dwelt in by generations as new. You may come into town
by the Mitcham bus. You find brown, black or red trams
waiting for you in a very narrow Square of old, but not ancient,
untidy, and probably 'doomed' shops. Rows of the small, red-
brick, slate-roofed houses, with bow windows to suggest a
certain superiority, run at right angles to the highway. They
whirl round and out of sight, as the tram advances, each moving
vista ending in the screen of distant trees. Suddenly, on the
highroad itself, there is a long block of buildings, white, and
with green shutters above, liver-coloured brick below, slate
roofed, rather startling and rather impressive. A high paling and
a few tall elms still on the road-line, announce that this, too,
was, till the other day, an old estate. A large, lettered, black
board spells out that here are the County Council's workmen's
dwellings and attempt to solve the housing question. What shall
be the defects of their qualities, no doubt Time, with the

revolution of her wheel, will bring to light. Perhaps the County Council will be forced to play the part of the squire of country villages, to insist that the tenants' floors are washed, and the faces of their children, and that may be an interference with the liberty of the subject. But for the moment these houses, empty still, clean still, and standing on a green field, are stimulating, and, as I have said, impressive. Electric trams are to link this village of so many thousand, let into a district of a million or so, with Westminster, with Blackfriars, and with London Bridge.

There are ancient houses, late Georgian, that peer, as if querulously, over the side hoardings. They seem to gloom* behind high walls, in the shadow of tall trees, at the end of black gardens. They are painted white, with glass excrescences, observatories, perhaps, on their roofs among the chimneys and boughs. Once they were the considerable houses of an exclusive village. They were built when macadam roads had gradually become practicable for carriages of the leisured and the well off. Now the County Council houses and their trams shall, in the same spot, serve the hurried and the not rich, by right of roads.

Touching these few houses is a short, more modern but still old, double line of shops. The more reputable touch the most jumbled; they have been made by building sale rooms out over old gardens, from small groundfloors to the line of the pavement, – old-curiosity shops, rag and bone shops, the queer, grimy, sometimes astonishingly 'old established', sometimes very transitory little odds-and-ends shops (where the servants of the well-off sell old 'Time's', and kitchen grease, and where workmen buy second-hand tools and old blankets) of the outlying districts. They will disappear, I suppose, soon enough, move further out, and continue their individual, ratlike, and very useful existences.

Almost immediately afterwards there are long 'parades' of shops, stores, emporia, all terracotta, plate glass, soft stone and gilt letters. Crowds move slowly in front of these – it is not possible to hurry even on the broad pavements, and most people move leisurely, with the head a little to one side, looking at the large windows, carrying parcels. Then there are more old houses behind old trees, or behind little terraces, then, more new shops. A brand new theatre, immense, domed, suddenly holds aloft, at its very apex, a large allegorical figure that appears on the point to soar over all these buildings and all these people. It is startling, because one does not expect the spectacular; it suggests the domed, statue-crowned brown stone buildings that in Strasburg* the Prussians have erected to flaunt in front of the gracious French château of the governor of Alsace-Lorraine.

The effect in London is just as much one of jumble and the incongruous, but there is nothing of the sinister. If it is not an impression of pure happiness it certainly implies a contagious cheerfulness and good humour. In these parts you hardly see a discontented face, and never a morbid one. Right in to the very bottom of the Waterloo Road, and nearly up to Westminster Bridge, old villas, new houses and new shops lie side by side, or stare at one another. They are all mixed together, it is not possible to get any zones to 'synchronise', it is not possible to say 'early Georgian London had reached here, middle Victorian here, the railways produced this district, the short stages this'. They are dropped down in terraces anywhere, nearer Whitehall, or further away. But the general effects is a pleasant one. It is as if the poorer classes had come into the cast-off clothes of the comfortable, and found them roomy, easy and luxurious.

I suppose the speculative builder accounts for this. He found in one generation or the other, bits of waste ground, or rows of smaller buildings; he ran up at one time the fine old houses, at another the terra cotta shops. Probably in each case he was miscalled by the old residents; so does the 'jerry built'* terrace of the late Georges become the pathetic old region of today; so no doubt the new shops will, to our children's children, be tenderly reminiscent, quaint, and full of old memories; so does Time assuage all temporal griefs.

The speculative builder's lamentable failures may be traced too. There is an odd terrace in one part of a long main road into London, it contains four immense, thin-walled, pretentious stucco houses, with middle Victorian pinnacles, gables and extravagances. It breaks off in uncompleted doors, uncompleted foundations, and a plot of grimy waste land. Other shops begin again. This place always piques my curiosity. I seem to trace in it a bold speculation's falling to pieces, getting the nickname 'Blank's Folly', growing begrimed, being forgotten.

These great roads into London are pleasant enough, inspiring too and impressive when they are full of people. In the times when one is in the mood, when one is 'looking' – and at such times the top of the horse-drawn tram is the best of all vehicles

– one sees glimpses of so many things that it is like sitting before an unending stage procession, only more actual, more pathetic and much more inspiring. The other year I came in by way of the Kennington Road; along Newington Butts, past the Elephant,* up London Road our eyes had grown accustomed to a gloom in the upper air. The Obelisk milestone in St George's Circus* appeared, pallid under its lamps, pale and grimy, Georgian, grim and surprising; the tall wedge of the Eye Hospital was a deep black among liquid shadows deeper still. All the mysterious and gloomy London of ancient names and ancient lives seemed converging out of those shadows into that dark space. And suddenly, at a swinging round of the tram, there was a long trail of quivering lamps, pink, red, and white, low down on the ground, vanishing in the distance of Waterloo Road.

The road was 'up' for putting down the conduits of the electric system, and these lights guarded the trenches. But there had been no announcement, no expectation of a city rejoicing with illuminations; it was the most gracious of surprises and an unforgettable thing. But that is London.

Yet these great roads are oppressive when they are empty. To enter London in a faint, saffron dawn, along with the market wagons, is to be not awed by an immense humanity but disturbed by entering what seems some realm of the half supernatural. You are coming to Covent Garden, you sit at the shaft-tail beside the driver, he is half invisible in the night, taciturn and half asleep. At last the street lamps appear, at first solitary and brave in the dark, then more frequent and growing palely unnatural before the dawn; the colours of the large horses begin to show, and the innumerable 'pulls up', with their signposts and the yellow paint of the housefacings. Or you may lie softly enough high up on a bed of cabbages.

There used to be at the back of the Camden Town Road a little hay market that I knew well – it may be there still for all I know – and it was far better to come in on top of the hay, half under the tarpaulin, with the sweet scent, the warmth and the half dozing, the pure air of the early dawn. It is purest of all on a Monday, because fewer chimneys have been smoking. One saw the solitary streets for immense distances with, all along the roadways, little heaps that turned out to be cats crouching over garbage or courting; they are the sign visual of London at the dawn, with an air of mystery as of an unsuspected population revealed unawares. But all the empty streets giving out echoes that one never hears during the day, all the vacant blinds, the sinister, the jocular, the lugubriously inquiring, or the lamentable expressions that windows give to houses asleep, all the unsmoking chimneys, the pale skies, and the thought of all these countless thousands lying invisible, with their souls, in sleep, parted from their bodies – all those things give an effect, in its silence, immense, stealthy, and overpowering.

One coffee-stall, grey-hooded and with a pale lamp, does not break the spell, nor twenty; one house of call, nor a hundred. Even the shouts of Covent Garden or the footsteps on the cobbles, and the undertones of the loafers before the tiny black brick houses of the little hay market, seem thin and ghostly without the immense and kindly ground-bass of London awake. And, indeed, all the dawn sounds of London have that quality of thinness – the hoot of locomotives, the thunder peals of shunting trucks, the clatter of cab-horse hoofs, the rhythmical stepping of one's own four great horses. Even the immensely loud awakening of the London birds seems small and circumscribed.

The railways seem to make London commence where the chimney pots begin to be in forests. In comparison with the Thames they are at the other end of the scale. The River is a natural way; roads wind upon hills, descend valleys in zig-zags, make nowadays detours that were once necessary in order to strike fords or to convenience great houses or solitary hamlets. Railroads tunnel through hills, fill up valleys with embankments and crash through the town itself, boring straight ways into the heart of it with a fine contempt for natural obstacles.[1] If we

---

[1] Canals have something of this quality, and in them it is of older date. Brindley* carried the Bridgewater canal over a river by means of an iron bridge in the days when men still wore tie wigs and dress swords. I do not touch on this kind of road into London because it is no longer a very usual one. At one time it was common enough. I remember to have read an account in verse, by a starving and permanently obscure eighteenth-century poet, of a voyage he made from London to Nottingham and back with his entire family, a wife and six children. He was seeking a patron, but finding none he printed this pamphlet and hawked it through the streets. I am familiar enough with several canals. When I was a boy I persuaded a bargee to take me through the tunnel that goes under the Edgware Road and reappears near Regent's Park. The darkness, the

could see the underlying fineness of these things, the fineness that shall be on the surface when these embankments are as venerable as today the wall of Hadrian,* it might make our world more inspiring. There are deep cuttings, coming into London where brick walls, fifty feet high, are black, sombre, and austere. You are in a kind of underworld, savagely impressive enough. The square fronts of houses peep down on you as you run beneath; constant footbridges overhead give to the thin light of day a constant shudder and quiver. We, who are not made for strong impressions, are ourselves inclined to shudder.

Or one may grow bewildered to the point of losing hold of one's identity amid the crash and charge of goods trucks. There are great open spaces all over London where the transfers are made from line to line. At night they are most active. Electric lights glare and seem to drop sparks from very high in the air, blue and mistily; rails glimmer here and there underfoot like marsh pools of water; hooded trucks seem to wander alone and to charge each other in all the black distances. One might be on some primæval plain, watching, in the glare of lightning, to the unceasing crash of thunder, primordial beasts grazing, wandering, or in violent combat. Yet at these things, too, we are apt to shudder, as in his day Horace disliked the Via Flaminia.*

Or we cry out: 'These things are bringing in the millennium.' Perhaps they are. To really descend, not in body alone, but with the spirit receptive, into this whirl and crash, to see men running with set faces, at the continual risk of their lives, that they may link up wagons, bringing screws from Birmingham, corn from Canada, pine-planks from Norway, pork from the United States, to whirl oneself in the whirl of it, is to be overcome with convictions. We live in spacious times. Humanity is on the march somewhere, tomorrow the ultimate questions shall be solved and the soul of man assuaged. Perhaps it shall. It is possible in the contagion of these things to see the opening up of Empires wider of sway than Rome, clearer of sight than Greece, kinder of heart than Carthage,* purer in joy than was

---

plash of waters, the faint stars of light at either end, combined to make a deep impression on me. The bargee and his mate pushed themselves and the barge along by pressing their bare feet against the walls of the tunnel.

to be had among the hanging gardens of Babylon.* Or is this only rhetoric, or only romance?

For myself, when on a train into London, I feel almost invariably a sense of some pathos and of some poetry. To the building up of this railway, of this landscape of roofs, there went so many human lives, so much of human endeavour, so many human hopes. Small houses, like the ranks of an infinite number of regiments caught in the act of wheeling, march out upon the open country; in the mists of the distance they climb hills, and the serrated roofs look like the jagged outlines of pinewoods with, at the top, the thin spike of a church tower. The roofs come closer together; at last, in their regular furrows, they present the appearance of fields ploughed in slate, in tiles, in lead, with the deeper channels of the streets below. Certain details strike at the eye: parallel lines of white cement set diagonally in the slate courses whirl past, bewilderingly, like snow in a wind; lines of rails shoot suddenly from beneath the embankments; and, rather surprisingly, bits of black field lie in the very heart of it all, with cabbages growing, and a discoloured donkey tethered to a peg. The plain of roof tops broadens out again. Perhaps the comparative quiet fosters one's melancholy. One is behind glass as if one were gazing into the hush of a museum; one hears no street cries, no children's calls. And for me at least it is melancholy to think that hardly one of all these lives, of all these men, will leave any trace in the world. One sees, too, so many little bits of uncompleted life. As the train pauses one looks down into a main street – and all streets are hardly recognizable from a height. A bus is before the steps of a church, a ragged child turns a catherine wheel in the road, and holds up her hand to the passengers. Suddenly a blue policeman steps into the roadway. The train moves on.

The other day, too, we were moving rather slowly. I looked down upon black and tiny yards that were like the cells in an electric battery. In one, three children were waving their hands and turning up white faces to the train; in the next, white clothes were drying. A little further on a woman ran suddenly out of a door; she had a white apron and her sleeves were tucked up. A man followed her hastily, he had red hair, and in his hand a long stick. We moved on, and I have not the least idea whether he were going to thrash her, or whether together they were going to beat a carpet. At any rate, the evening papers reported no murder in Southwark.

Incidents even so definite as these are more or less the exception, but the constant sucession of much smaller happenings that one sees, and that one never sees completed, gives to looking out of train windows a touch of pathos and of dissatisfaction. It is akin to the sentiment ingrained in humanity of liking a story to have an end. And it is the 'note' of all roads into London.

To indulge in the feeling to any extent would be to add a new morbidity to life. One would, quite literally, never get any for'arder if one stayed to inquire to the end of every tragicomedy of which, on one's road, one caught a glimpse. And it is unpractical to wish that every bricklayer and mortar carrier who added his wall to the infinite number already existing should be able to sign his work as an artist signs his picture. But that, too, is a universal sentiment and a 'note' of all roads into London, a note of London itself. It arises out of the innate altruism that there is in us all, or out of the universal desire to 'know'.

If one stayed to think, one would like to know what kind of poor wretch set the fifth stone in the third tier of the Pyramid of Cheops.*

CHAPTER 3

Work in London

The Thames is the oldest, as it is the most majestic of the roads into London, but its character as a road is obscured, justly enough. Along the others we travel to reach our work, our love, to meet our death. Along the Thames those who travel are working always, the passengers it bears leave it at the very gates of London.

Gravesend, with its high front of piers characteristic in their dark and rigid architecture of piles, is a place of romance to the sailor who comes to London from the deep waters. It is the signal that, after his ninety days of empty sea and empty sky, he has come very near to his harbours. Sailors speak of the place with the remembrance of old and good times, giving a soft look to the eyes, a soft tone to the voice; they are the look and tone of those who think about old emotions, of pleasure, of impatience, of the times when they said 'Only a day more now.' The river front of Gravesend means that.

On the other bank a square, large red hotel faces these pile structures across the broad gray sweep of water and air. It marks the gates of the lowest docks, and here, for the river, psychological London begins. It does not much matter whether the ship turns in there at Tilbury or whether it works up to the docks in Gallions Reach, or to the others in the heart of town itself. Work for them ends there.

It is taken up by the red-sailed barges. They tack in their engrossed manner across and across the wide reaches; they pass under the shadow of dull clouds, of rain squalls, under watery sunlight, the arms of aligned cranes, the smoke from factory chimneys. They linger, going about, in front of bluffs covered with gray buildings and black trees; in exposed stretches of water they are covered, right over the hatches, by the wash from the sea-tarnished sides of steamers so vast, so silent in their motions, so centred in themselves, that as, from the deck of a barge, one looks at their passing, it is hard to realise that they and not the low banks that they obscure and seem to swallow up, are gliding by.

These barges running up from Rotherhithe or from much farther out to sea, pass cement factories, sand works, anchored groups of skiffs where sand is hauled laboriously in buckets from the bottom of the river; they pass petroleum depôts where, side by side, gray retorts are like those of gas works; they pass candle factories and manure warehouses. They tack about gravely one after another beside a black smallpox hospital that, out in the river, is one half ship and the other a pier with a dingy and mournful resemblance to those of fashionable watering places. They move, these barges, in squadrons in a continual and mazy slant, red sail cutting diagonally across red sail, with here and there a large rent, and here and there a white patch. They give the 'character' to this road into London, to this river of toil. Their only rivals are the sludge boats, a fleet of large steamers owned by the County Council. These are running in a continuous string; they go swiftly down stream, low in the water, and showing all black. They come back empty, so high in the bows that a great streak of red shows from the keel upwards; they swing round in front of one or other of the sewage works, ready to take in another cargo to drop into the sea beyond the Nore as soon as the tide serves. The barges, however, carry coke, carry sand, carry gravel, and a hundred other things. Occasionally one loaded very high with a stack passes them all, looking for all the world like a man buried beneath a haycock; occasionally these, too, are passed by very gaily painted, astonishingly swift, racing barges, that thread the close traffic like brilliant shuttles, and roar and rustle through the water.

So at last, keeping out of the way of the sludge boats, out of the way of powder barges, of great steamers of the famous Lines, of swift fish carriers that raise an enormous wash, and of the Belle steamers that they detest most of all, the small flotillas come to the top of Tipcock Reach. Hitherto the factories have been scarce, mostly unsavoury and solitary. But a beacon rises up beyond the wharf of a powder factory that faces a manure warehouse. This beacon is spindly, tall, of iron lattice work. And all beyond it the river runs as between high walls, shining with a more metallic glitter under smoke and the shadows of groves of masts, crane-arms, chains, cordage. A train of the large steamers lies heavy on the water, hooting signals to agents ashore, waiting at the dock gates for water enough to enter. This is Gallions Reach, and from here upwards London offers a solid black facing to its river. From here, too, the little companies of barges begin to break up. Some stop near the dock gates, some turn into the London canals. Some wait near Waterloo, some go far above the bridges. Here at any rate the river as a road into London ends. It is all the time a gray tide of work, a moving platform of workers.

Workers in London divide themselves, roughly, into those who sell the labour of their bodies and those who sell their attentions. You see men in the streets digging trenches, pulling stout wires out of square holes in pavements, pecking away among greasy vapours at layers of asphalte, scattering shovelfuls of crushed gravel under the hoofs of slipping horses and under the crunching tyres of wheels. If walls would fall out of offices you would see paler men and women adding up the records of money paid to these others. That, with infinite variations, is work in London.

You get the two things united here and there. The other day I was in Tilbury Docks. (It is difficult to get away from this river.) The vast, empty squares of water lay parapeted, arbitrary and dim in their eternal perspectives; the straight lines of the water, the straight lines of the parapets, of the bottoms of the goods sheds, of the tops, of the gray corrugated roofs, all dwindled together into the immense and empty distances. The rows of four-footed, gaunt, inactive cranes, painted a dull rust colour, and the few enormous steamers at the inner ends of the quays – all these things were wetted, fused and confused in their outlines, beneath a weeping sky in which a drapery of clouds had the look of a badly blotted water-colour painting, still wet and inefficient. Knots of stevedores in dim and neutral coloured clothes seemed to be doing nothing perfunctorily in the shadow of the great hulls.

A big, red faced, heavy-moustached man in blue clothes and with cheerfully brass-bound cap and shoulders, hurried out of a tin shed. It was labelled: 'Office of the Steam Navigation Co.' He slipped hastily between the black side of one of the huge sheds and a gray, rusty and sea-fretted liner. Her lower sides gaped in large holes screened with canvas, and from moment to moment obscured by grimy buckets of coal that rose from a lighter; her square, white upper deck cabins were being painted more white by painters in white jackets. He hurried very fast, with a masterful and engrossed step, a cheerful blue figure with pink cheeks, dodging mechanically the pools of greasy water and the fat black mud between the sleepers. He dived into another small office. He was the chief officer of the liner that was coaling and he had a pencil behind his ear.

He was uniting as it were the labours of the men shovelling in the buckets of coal, of the men uttering melancholy wails as they swung-in a white boat, of the men hooking up long planks for the painters to sit on, and of the painters themselves on the upper decks. With that pencil he controlled all their labours, as if he were twisting them into an invisible rope which passed through that tin office and up, far away into town where other pencils and other pens recorded these things on large pages, digested them into summaries and finally read them out to Boards of Directors.

Those invisible ropes — they are strong enough in all conscience — seem to be the only tie between these two classes of workers, between these two great camps set one against another. It is astonishing how different London looks from one or from the other end. Speaking broadly, the man who expresses himself with a pen on paper sees his London from the west. At the worst he hopes to end with that view. His London of breathing space, his West End, extends from say Chiswick to say Portland Place. His dense London is the City as far as Fenchurch Street, his East End ends with what he calls 'Whitechapel'.

The other sees his London of elbow room extend from say Purfleet to say Blackwall. He is conscious of having, as it were at his back, the very green and very black stretches of the Essex marshes dotted with large solitary factories and small solitary farms. His dense London, *his* City, lies along the line from Blackwall to Fenchurch Street. Beyond that, the City proper, the city of the Bank and the Mansion House, is already a place rather of dilettante trifling. Its streets are tidied up, its buildings ornamented and spacious. The end of the West End is for him the Piccadilly Fountain,* and this latter quarter of large, almost clean, stone buildings, broad swept streets and a comparative glare of light, is already a foreign land, slightly painful because it is so strange. That, further west, there may be another enormous London never really enters his everyday thoughts. He reads about it sometimes, he hears it spoken of; sometimes perhaps in a holiday frame of mind he goes through it. But it never 'matters' to him, it is never like his familiar, rigid rows of streets all of blackened bricks, windows that are square openings in boxes and plasters of blue and white and begrimed enamelled iron advertisements. These are familiar, these are real life, these are homely, as if warm and alive. The other he does not much want to think about, it would worry him. In just the same way the penworker does not want to think about several dark towns of a million or so east of 'Whitechapel'. It is an unpleasant thought. Given ill-luck, a craving for drink, disease or one or other of the fatal falls of humanity, he too might have to sink into those gloomy and shadowy depths. The other man is vaguely troubled at the idea of the West. There he would have to be tidy, constrained, worried about specks on his clothes, careful of his tongue, less than a man.

These two types, in their mass very human and very comprehensible, are in general very foreign and in general very hostile the one to the other. Yet upon their combined workings the life of London depends. And because there they may work one into another like the teeth of cogwheels revolving antithetically, London attracts them. For the obvious secret of London, its magnetism, is the work that it offers to be done or to be 'organised'. You go there whether you got your training at the tail of a plough in Kent or in Lithuania, with the most salient fact in your experience the knowledge of a pollard willow in which there is always a dog-fox asleep; or whether beside the Isis, on the links of St Andrews,* or in the University of Bonn you learnt the sorrows of Achilles,* the binomial theorem, or the chemical formulae of all the coal tar by-products. You go there, whether your ideal is to get a wage of fifteen shillings a week more with lighter work and shorter hours, or whether you dream that before 'retiring' you will get yourself turned into a limited company with a capital of six cyphers at the tail of a numeral – you go there to get 'something to do'. That is the grosser view.

But the finer side is the romantic, the adventurous, the dreamer's spirit in mankind to whom work itself in imagination remains the primal curse. In certain cellars here and there in the City, in cellars that have been oil-clothed and tiled, garnished with rows of hat-pegs and with leather seats like planks along the walls, above white marble table-tops that loom like horizontal tombstones through the delicate films of cigarette smoke, contending in the dim atmosphere with the delicate fragrance of coffee – in a City Mecca,* in fact – you will see men sit. Their faces of the palest, of the ruddiest, of the blondest, of the most black-avised, will be all united into one serious frown over black and white stones, like smaller tombstones standing or lying prone as if in a disastrously wrecked graveyard. A man will rise in a far corner, pull the lapels of his coat one towards another, shake his umbrella a little, and walk away with a swift step and a half self-conscious air. A young man will look up and lose for a moment his engrossed expression. He will stop his companion's domino in mid air with 'Do you know who that is? Why, Plumly!' – 'What, Plumly of the Dash United?' They will gaze with half awe at the disappearing trouser-ends and boot-heels on the stairs.

'Yes. Plumly was only an auctioneers' clerk in Honiton, where my father is. And now look what he's worth! That was what made me come to town.' The eyes of both young men will have serious and reflective expressions before they resume their game. They will both be thinking, in one way or another, that what man has done man can do.

Or, on the seat before the ferryman's hut in a small harbour you may see a hook-nosed, bearded, begrimed, weather-soiled and wonderfully alert London bargeman. He will wave his tiny pipe at the faces of half a dozen young fishermen standing in a circle before him.

'Yes,' he will say, 'you're too young to remember Johnston. But his mother and Mrs Spence, who keeps the "Blue William" here, were first cousins . . . Bill Johnston of the "Britisher".'

Bill Johnston of the 'stumpy' called 'Britisher' had in his childhood sailed from that port aboard a coaling schooner. Afterwards he had 'been South', he had been in the Cape Mounted Police, then he had returned to London. He had saved a little money and bought a share in his 'stumpy', which is a barge without a topsail: he had carried freight unceasingly from Rotherhithe into the Pool or into the canals; his employers had advanced him money to buy the barge outright; he had carried freights until he had paid them back. 'And now,' his eulogiser comments, 'he sails that there river, Bill Johnston, with his missis for mate and his kid for apprentice; he's in his own home with a cooking range in the cabin and a joint hanging in the hatchway for a larder. He's his own master; he comes when he will and he goes; he draws a steady three quid a week, and he's buying up other barges gradual.'

The young fishermen standing round dive their hands deeper into their russet breeches pockets and gaze out over the rubble of old boats, cork floats, harbour mud and piles. The old man sucks at his pipe, spits, waves a grimy hand wanting a thumb, and says, 'Just such a lad as you be Bill Johnston were,' and a boy moves his hands in his pockets sighing 'Ah!'

You will see scenes just the same besides the Bay of Naples and, *mutatis mutandis*,* in Ukrainia and the Levant. For London calls out across the lands to the spirit of Romance, to the spirit of youth and the spirit of adventure – to the Finer Spirits.

There are such glorious plums. And the thought of them eventually fills alike those City Meccas and the square, blackened brick, balconied dock-dwellings; it fills the bare rooms in Whitechapel, where dark and hook-nosed men sit amid the stench of humanity, their mouths filled with small brass nails, silent amid the rattling clatter of hammers on boot soles. It fills, too, the behind-counters of large drapers, the very sewers with large neutral-coloured scavengers, and the great Offices in Whitehall. In the whitewashed and grimy courts of Saffron Hill splendid-limbed, half-nude children tumble, dark eyed, like the cherubs of Cinquecento* pictures, round the feet of dark men puffing cigarette smoke, and fair Venetian girls lean back, smiling and chattering, in bright head-cloths, bright neck-cloths, bright bodices and bright petticoats against brilliant barrows. Hook-nosed, saturnine and imperturbable old men mix, with the air of sorcerers, flour, vanilla, cochineal, and condensed milk in pewter freezing pots like infernal machines. The Finer Spirit . . . because, today as always and for ever, the streets of London are paved with gold.

I remember reading somewhere a long time ago an ingenious article pronouncing boldly that this splendid figure of speech, this myth shining down the ages, was literally true. I remember the bare existence of the article, but I cannot remember its arguments. It was, perhaps, because the ground in front of the Mansion House is worth its area in sovereigns set on edge. Or it may have been that, according to the writer, the mud trodden underfoot was, for some profound chemical reason, worth its weight in gold. In either case a favoured few do undoubtedly possess the secret of alchemy, in that everything they touch – mud, too, no doubt – turns to gold. And the number of that favoured few is very great, because in London there are so many things to touch. Hence the immensity of London's silent appeal. She calls to all the world.

'In the old days', there were, say, The Holy Land,* the 'Wars' where thousands of mercenaries cut by turns the throats of Ferrarese, of Bolognese, of French, of Burgundians, of Kaiserliks* and of each other. There were afterwards the Indies, Peru, Mexico, the Spanish Main; then more Wars of Seven, of Thirty years' duration* – then the opening up of the silent East, then goldfields. These things called to the adventurous of succeeding generations for ten centuries. But these appeals were limited. They called only to those who felt able to handle a sword, fire a thatch, cut the rings off a woman's hand, set a sail, shoot in a wood, march a thousand miles or come out of a death of thirst. They were for the valorous alone who could work with their hands.

The appeal of London is far wider. She has seemed for the last century or so to stand on high, offering, like the figure on the Duke of York's column,* laurel wreaths to all the world. She seems to hold them for bank clerks and for bargees, for charlatans and the Founders of Faiths, to poets and to privates in the Foot Guards, to actors as to all sorts of robbers with violence. But the appeal is on the whole a modern one: it was not until the wider world of woods and seas was nearly all exploited that the Occidental peoples 'discovered' London. To enter minutely into this movement would be impracticable. It would take one very deep into that odd psychology of statistics that is called Political Economy.

But it had its rise, this modern appeal of London, at about the time of the triumphing principle of Free Trade;[1]* it had its

---

[1] I have, however, just read the book of a well received Political Economist who asserts that it did not. The modern spirit is by him attributed to the 'consistent, unrelenting, true-sighted policy of five centuries of English Governmental action to a protective system which, in fact, was only relaxed when the supremacy had been reached'. It isn't, of course, my business to assert the one or the other dogma. The supremacy of London's particular attraction came at about the time of Free Trade. But Free Trade itself may have come

beginning at about the time when the world evolved the equally triumphant principles of Limited Liability, Specialism in Labour and the freedom of knowledge.

It was probably foreshadowed in the opening years of last century by the triumphant figure of Napoleon I.* He more than anyone stands for that other triumphant principle: What man has done man can do. He raised the standard of the adventurer not only towards respectability but towards apotheosis.

Before his day the great London adventurers were, actively, the Drakes and the Raleighs; passively, Casanovas and Cagliostros. Roderick Random's* idea of 'making a career' after the Wars had failed him, was to pretend in London to be a man of fashion, to victimise an heiress, or in some miraculous way to pick up a 'patron' with influence. There was not in those days any other career in the Town. Macshanes, O'Creegans, an occasional Colonel Evans, perhaps a French barber spying in the service of the Pretender, a few poets like Thomson of the 'Seasons' and a few bastards like Tom Jones* – all these people were obsessed by these two ideas. They sat in their best clothes toying with their snuff-boxes or ostentatiously winding up jewelled watches in boxes at the Opera; they panted to attract the attention of an heiress or they wrote dedications and fee'd the footmen of peers.

It would be fanciful to make Buonaparte too responsible for the Modern Type; but he, upon the whole, was the discoverer

---

because just then London had become supreme owing to five centuries of Protection. Or the reverse may have been the case.

Both are possible enough, because in the arena of Triumphant Principle pendulums swing backwards and forwards: the undisputed right of today becoming the open question of tomorrow, and the unquestioned wrong of the immediate future. That is a platitude because it is one of the indisputable verities. In the country they say that large clocks when they tick solemnly and slowly, thud out the words: 'Alive – Dead; Alive – Dead' – because in this world at every second a child is born, a man dies. But, in London, a listener to the larger clock which ticks off the spirits of successive ages, seems to hear above the roar of the traffic, the slow reverberation: 'Never – Again; Never – Again', as principles rise and die, and rise and die again. For in London that fact forces itself upon the ear and upon the eye; it is a part of the very dust. It is, perhaps, the final lesson of the great, human place. Arts rise and die again, systems rise and die again, faiths are born only to die and to rise once more; the only thing constant and undying is the human crowd.

of the principle: apply yourself to gain the affection of the
immense crowd. After his day the mere heiress and the patron
as ends of a career vanish. They remain merely as stepping
stones.

But the immense crowd is still the indubitable end. If hardly
any of us aspire to its suffrage in its entirety, we have, in London
at least, discovered the possibilities of capturing its custom in its
smallest trifles. To make a corner in collar studs would be rather
American: the method in London is to invent, or to buy up the
invention of, a collar stud that will appeal straight to the heart
of the million, a collar stud that will be not only in all the street
vendors' trays, but in all the barbers', all the hosiers', all the
drapers' windows. It ought to be very cheap, very picturesquely
'put on the market', and just perishable enough to make a
constant supply desirable. The man who did put it on the market
would immediately become the Napoleon of the Collar Stud.

There are already so many of these: there is at least one, I am
not sure that there are not several, of the Press; Napoleons of
the Lower Finance find their Waterloos every few years. There
is a Napoleon of Pharmacy, one of the Tea Trade, one of
Grocery, one of Underclothing. This is not a mere figure of
speech on my part: the words are used month by month by each
of these Trade Journals. There is very obviously one of politics,
but that 'career', as things are in London of today, has become
comparatively decorative – a hobby for Napoleons in retire-
ment. What one would sigh for is no longer the making of a
people's laws or of a people's songs, but of a people's socks.
With that behind one, one may die Chancellor of the Exchequer
and a peer of the realm.

This obviously is desirable enough; we sigh very reasonably
for business men in our cabinets. It is picturesque too, and
inspiring, it brings about kaleidoscopic changes, and the wildest
of contrasts. It makes life more worth living, because it makes
life more interesting, and more amusing. The trouble, the defect
of this particular Quality, is that the work suffers. The workers
and their immediate dependants suffer perhaps still more.

The two clerks in that City Mecca – I happened to be
watching them – saw that particular millionaire cross through
the cigarette smoke and disappear. He, too, was a Napoleon of
a particular financial order, and those two young men, when
they rose from their dominos, pulled together their coats, shook

their umbrellas a very little, and set their hats on at a particular angle. They were imitating almost gesture for gesture their hero.

I have no means of knowing how much further in the real mysteries of his craft they imitated him. I do not know whether they possessed his tremendous energy, his industry, his nerve, his knowledge of the market – whether they possessed even a shade of his temperament. It is obvious, however, that the great majority do not, that the chance against any average young man is a 'thousand to one'. I used to know rather intimately a talented and in that sense romantic young man, whom I will call X. X had several irons in the fire: that meant that he had several Napoleons he could imitate. He had a very reasonable competence: he invested it in a certain wholesale business, of which he knew little more than that fortunes were rapidly made in it. He occupied certain offices which looked down on Aldgate* Pump.

The rooms appealed to his romanticism: he found it extremely picturesque to see women, actually with pails, in London, in the twentieth century, really fetching water. It was interesting, too, to look at the Trade Papers, and his office had lockers all round it. They were meant to contain samples of the raw material he traded in. I happened once to open one; it revealed rather astonishingly the tinfoil necks of champagne bottles.

X sanguinely and amiably explained. Strauss, an awfully sharp man, the Napoleon of the . . . Trade, had his lockered office just round the corner: he always offered his clients – perhaps 'suitors' would be the right word – that particular brand of wine. He kept it in just such a receptacle.

That part of the business X attended to with amiability and success: he had also an idea that the Banks were advancing his partner money on some sort of 'cover system'; the crop somewhere in the East was going to fail: his partner – X financed this partner – had taken care to be early in the market: as soon as the season commenced they would be making a profit of £90 a week, and with a few more such lucky specs, X would be able to clear out with £50,000.

He attended at his office thus amiably, he wrote an occasional letter on his typewriter, which was rather fun, he looked out of window at the Pump, he countersigned cheques, and genially acknowledged that the . . . Trade was full of rogues, from ten until four.

Then he hurried westwards to his large white and ormolu*

house, and sat down to a rosewood Chippendale* bureau. He had there another Napoleon before his eyes.

This was a celebrated novelist, who made £7,000 a year, by dictating topical novels into a phonograph. X accordingly dictated topical novels – when the war broke out,* a romance of South Africa; during the Chinese Massacres,* a Chinese novel.

He displayed an astonishing industry over this speculation, and, having devoted his two or three hours a day to it, he 'dressed', and with his wife, either dined out, or 'dined' other amiable and fashionable persons. That, too, was part of the game, because to get on in either the Book or the other Trade, you have to 'know people'. Sometimes after returning from the opera X would sit down and write a topical critique and sketch – he had a talent for sketching – the dresses and the *mise en scène.** This was because he knew a Journalist – a Napoleon of the Paragraph – who said he made £4,000 a year at similar odd moments.

But I never heard X attach any importance to knowing how to 'write', or to learning the ins and outs of the . . . Trade. He had his irons, however, in these fires. His partner might scoop the market with Bosnians* when the Honduras crop failed, or X himself might make a hit with a novel. Either would mean a swift and easy affluence.

There is nothing inherently impossible in X's ideals, just as there is nothing criminal or mean. He represents, rather diffusely, the Modern Spirit. For, speaking largely, we in London today see life as a great gamble, London as a vast Monte Carlo, or, if you will, an immense Hamburg lottery. We put in a quite small stake, we may win a six figure lot. That is why London attracts us so supremely. If we do not at once win, we put in another small stake, and we continue until either we win, or our capital, our energy, our health, our youth, or our taste for gambling, come to an end.[1] This tendency is, in fact, a trade

---

[1] I do not of course mean that steady work is no longer to be found in the town of London. The industrious apprentice still climbs as he did in the time of Hogarth. But the essential 'note' of those who stand out among workers in modern London, appears on the surface to be that of gambling. That, in fact, is the most striking note of work in modern London, it is in that that it differs from work in all past Londons, and it is that which is the pre-eminent attractiveness of London itself. There is obviously mere work enough, sober and uninviting, to keep men in the country districts all over Europe.

custom, like any other: it is a vast frame of mind, that one may not like, but that one has not any valid ethical reason for condemning.

But the pity for X, as for so many other amiable and gallant young men, is that even in this modern market, the essentially old-fashioned must be to be found at the bottom of the sack. What work we do must still in one way or another be good in the sense of being attractive. You must still lay a good coin of some realm or other on the green cloth.

I know, for instance, another young man not so dilettante – neither indeed so charming nor so amiable as X – but almost more romantic. I will call him P. He had inherited a business of a specially old-established, a specially trustworthy, a specially eminent kind – one of those houses as reliable and as 'placed', as is Childs' in the banking, or Twinings'* in the tea trade. When P came into it, it was already beginning to feel the touch of competition from Stores. It had relied upon old-fashioned 'good' customers; it had never advertised.

P not only advertised generally and lavishly, but he put on the market cheap and attractively packed 'specialities'. He tried in fact to corner London's collar studs. What his business lost immediately in caste, he tried to make up at home. He devoted his leisure time to a species of scientific investigation connected with his trade, which along with Napoleons of Specialities, has room for disinterested and abstruse investigators with great names and no money – famous 'benefactors of their kind'. P, in fact, was making a large and romantic bid: he sacrificed the particular aroma of respectability of his business to a kind of large altruism: he sacrificed his great name in his trade organs, to the chance of gaining in the wider papers a considerable and undying fame. And this is very characteristic of the conditions of modern work in London. Our poets have to gain a daily bread in the public offices, our scientists in electric light works. We may all know an admirable critic of *belles lettres*: he gives eight hours of his day to checking the issue and return of dog licences at Somerset House, and there are many religious enthusiasts of the type of Swedenborg* who spend even longer hours in measuring and selling cheap ribbons. They are doing it in order on Sundays to preach in the parks.

London, in fact, if it make men eminently materialist in their working hours (and that is the great cry of all idealists against the great place), makes them by reaction astonishingly idealist in their interior souls. I know a railway signalman. He spends dreadfully long hours, high up in a sort of cage of wood and glass, above the innumerable lines of shimmering rails just outside the dim cave of a London's terminus. He works himself dog-tired, pulling levers that are constantly bright with the friction of his hands; he listens to the drilling sounds of little bells, straining his eyes to catch the red and white placards on the breasts of distant engines. At night in a cottage 'down the line' he spends more hours, making out of pith and coloured paper little models, like stalactite work, of the English Cathedrals. His small holidays go in making trips to Bath, to Exeter, to Durham, and his small savings are spent on architectural drawings and photographs of details. His ambition is to make a model of every cathedral in this country, and, if life holds out, of those at Rouen, Amiens, and Notre Dame de Paris.

This is an ideal: his eyes grow hazy and romantically soft at the thought of finally having in his working shed all these small white objects. But he does not in the least care about architecture. I once met by accident a man of forty, a cashier of a London bus company. He rather disliked the country, but his ambition was to cover, on his bicycle, every road of the United Kingdom. He inked over on his ordnance map each road that he travelled on, and he saw, in imagination, as a glorious finale like a dream, one of the sixpenny papers publishing a half-tone block representing this map with all its coach roads inked and distinct like the filaments of a skeleton leaf.

Collectors and connoisseurs there have been, no doubt, in all the ages since Nero* carried off his five hundred bronzes from Delphi. But the recreations of this signalman and this bus-cashier are simply mental anodynes: if they were not necessary for self-preservation they would be imbecile. The conditions of modern labour make them almost more than necessary. A man who retires from any routine work at all strenuous, signs nowadays his own death warrant if he have no hobby.

And all work in modern London is almost of necessity routine work: the tendency to specialise in small articles, in small parts of a whole, insures that. It becomes daily more difficult to find a watch operative who can make a timepiece, from escapement to case. One man as a rule renders true little cogwheels that have been made by machine, another polishes tiny pinion screws, another puts all these pieces together, another adjusts them. In just the same way one woman machines together trousers that have been roughly cut out by machine, another buttonholes them, another finishes them. And in just the same way in offices, a partner mentions the drift of a letter to a clerk, he dictates it to a shorthand-typewriter, she writes and addresses it, a boy posts it. And the clerk, the typewriter and the boy go on doing the same thing from the beginning of the working day to the end without interest and without thought.

In the minds of these workers, work itself becomes an endless monotony; there is no call at all made upon the special crafts-man's intellect that is in all the human race. It is a ceaseless strain upon the nerves and upon the muscles. It crushes out the individuality, and thus leisure time ceases to be a season of rest, of simple lying still and doing nothing. One needs, on the contrary, to asert one's individuality, and to still the cry of one's nerves. This leads to these hobbies which, psychologically considered, are a form of new work making some appeal to our special temperaments. In men this means, as a rule, some sport in which they have a chance of asserting an individual superior-ity, and women workers find their vent in personal adornments or housework.

But women workers, at any rate of the very poor, have not even this solace. I call to mind one in particular, and this was her life. She was married – or perhaps she was not married – to a waterside labourer who, when he could work, made fair money. As a rule, he suffered from chronic rheumatism, and was next door to a cripple. She had four children under nine. She was a dark, untidy-haired woman with a face much pitted by small pox, and she had a horribly foul tongue. The room looked out upon a boxlike square of livid brick yards, a table was under a window, a sugar box held coals. Another, nailed above the mantel, held bits of bread, a screw of tea in white paper, a screw of sugar in blue, and a gobbet of margarine in a saucer. When her man was in work or bad enough to be in hospital, when, at any rate, he was out of the house, there would be no coal in the one box because he was not crouching over the fire, and a bit of bacon in the other because there was no fuel to pay for. What he made went for the rent. There was nothing else in the room except a mattress and, on a damp and discoloured wall, a coloured mezzotint of Perdita,* the mistress of George IV. I do not know how she had come to be pasted up there.

Till the school bell rang the children worked at her side. I don't think they were ever either dressed for school or given breakfasts by her. She made matchboxes at 2¾d the 144, and it was wonderful to watch her working – engrossed, expressionless, without a word, her fingers moved deftly and unerringly, the light very dim, the air full of the faint sickly smell of paste and of the slight crackling of thin wood, and the slight slop-slopping of the pastebrush. Sometimes she would sigh, not sorrowfully, but to draw a deeper breath. It was the only sound that was at all arbitrary, the only variation in the monotony of her life, the only thing that distinguished her from a wonderfully perfect machine. Now and then a piece of the thin wood cracked along the line of a knot, but she showed no sign of exasperation.

Her husband, as a rule, sat in front of the fire; his right hand had lost two fingers, his others were too swollen to be able to catch hold of a paste-brush, he sucked silently at the end of an empty pipe. To me, however, – I used to stand in the doorway and watch – what was appalling was not the poverty. It was not the wretchedness, because, on the whole, neither the man or the woman were anything other than contented. But it was the dire speed at which she worked. It was like watching all the time some feat of desperate and breathless skill. It made one hold one's own breath.

In face of it any idea of 'problems', of solutions, of raising the submerged, or of the glorious destinies of humanity, vanished. The mode of life became, as it were, august and settled. You could not pity her because she was so obviously and wonderfully equipped for her particular struggle: you could not wish to 'raise' her, for what could she do in any other light, in any other air? Here at least she was strong, heroic, settled and beyond any condemnation.

As for ideals ... Looking at the matter from a broad field which includes Theocritus, Nietzsche, the Eastern question,* or a general election, she had not even ideas. She was an engrossed and admirable machine. But if you gave her 2¾d, the price of a gross of boxes – if you gave her time literally, she would utter long bursts of language that was a mixture of meaningless obscenities and of an old fashioned and formal English. She did not see why the Irish were allowed in Southwark, and she would

shoot forth a monologue of grievances against her husband's
mates, shouldering the poor old chap out of a job, and stealing
his 'bacca, and him next door to a cripple; she had stuck the
carving knife through the arm of a drunken man because he had
tried to come into her room one night when her man was in
hospital. She laughed hoarsely at the idea, and made feints with
her hands.

These topics seemed to come out of her as words come out of
certain machines, unnatural and disturbing. She had not much
desire to talk, her hands and eyes were continually going back
to her paste-brush. But as for ideals! She wanted to keep off the
rates; she wanted the Charity Organisation people, 'them
enquiry blokes', to keep away. She wanted her children to get
their schooling done and easy things up a bit, helping her with
the pasting. Above all she wanted the two lads to keep out of
bad ways, and the two gals not to be bad gals with these here
shiny top boots. She wanted them to stop indoors and paste
match boxes. Sooner than see them on the streets she would use
the carving knife to them; she had a sister a flower hand, making
artificial flowers, who had 'fallen'.

Those were her ideals. If you translate them into terms of
greater material prosperity you find them identical with anyone
else's. One desires for the later years of one's life a little ease.
She would have it when the law permitted her children to aid
her. One desires privacy when one suffers, she would have it if
the enquiry blokes would keep away. One desires that one's
children should grow in virtue.

I should say that she was as contented and as cheerful as
myself; she probably knew better than people more enlightened
and with higher ambitions, the truth of the saying that was
constantly on her lips, 'We can't b . . . well all have everything.'
And, as I have said, to be in her presence was to find all
'problems'. Police court missionaries, societies, and sisters of the
poor grow dim and childish along with the Modern Spirit itself.
It was like interviewing the bedrock of human existence in a
cavern deep in the earth. 'Influences' on the surface, busy about
raising her seemed to become mere whispers a long way above.
She supported them all.

As you went upstairs to her room you were presented with an
astonishing picture. (I was at the time looking for an investment,
and this house had been offered to me as producing a highly

desirable rental.) It had once been a model dwelling; the stairs were of stone, but the railings, the banisters, the panels of nearly all the doors, and sometimes the very doorposts, every cupboard and every shelf, had been chopped down for firewood. As I went up past all these open doors and ragged door holes, in absolutely every room there were women, sometimes several, sometimes several children, bending over tables or over old sugar cases, silently and with great swiftness making matchboxes, making umbrella tassels, running together cheap coats, making artificial flowers – the very poor.

The thought – or rather it was a sensation so irresistible as to be an obsession – that in all that district all the houses were as similar inside as their outsides were unvarying, the thought was more than overwhelming. To look at London from that grim warren was to have a foreground like an untidy and uninspired battle field in which the background of broad streets and fine gray buildings vanished to almost nothing. No cathedral spires and the turrets of no museums peeped over those serrated roofs.

That problem that is no problem – the matter of the very poor workers – becomes there the only question of London. It is not, unfortunately perhaps, one that we can write or think about with any amiable cocksureness. It is not, unfortunately, one that any one man, any ten, or any two hundred can even touch from the outside. All these districts are honeycombed with missions, brotherhoods, and organisations. But the solution must come from within, and, inside there, there is no movement and only work. It is, in fact, a problem to all human intents insoluble, precisely because this particular class of worker is composed of individuals who, through heredity, through 'type', through temperament, for a hundred predestined and tragic reasons, are absolutely incapable of creating Movements.

Their whole nerve force, and nearly all their thoughts are given to their work. They are the dust filtered down from all the succeeding dominant types,* they are the *caput mortuum** precisely because they are hopelessly old fashioned. They cannot combine, they have not any thoughts left for it; they could not strike because they have no means of communication; they are inarticulate.

They are forming, and they have been forming for years, an hereditary class. Education hardly touches their children. It means that for ten or eleven years the poor little things are made acquainted with facts, and are underfed, and that when they are fourteen they fall again to their parents. They learn no trade, they go apprentices to no craft. After a year or two of matchbox making the 'facts' of their instruction are worn down out of their minds.

And that very virtue of their mothers, that fierce determination to keep the little things 'respectable', means tying them more and more to their rooms. That particular striving, a fierce craze forkeeping the children straight, is an almost universal 'note', a dominant passion among the mothers of the very poor.

These, then, are the obverse and the reverse of the medal of work in London that appears to be so much of a gamble, that is really so fierce and so logical a struggle. For if we take X as paying too little attention to his actual work, we must think of this woman as paying too much.

Work in London today, if it have become in all its branches less of craft, depends more and more, if its worker is to make any individual success, on 'temperament'. Temperament in that particular sense we must take to mean the quality of inspiring confidence in one's employer or in one's customer. It is something akin to the artist's temperament, it is something akin to the charlatan's power to hypnotise mobs. The worker, if he is to rise out of the ruck, must impose his private personality upon a greater, or upon a lesser, public.

This tendency is most observable in the periodical press, that most enormous and most modern of industries. Here upon the whole the aesthetically intrinsic quality of the work offered by a young man does not matter much. The employer sits as it were in an office chair between the great public and the men who besiege him. It is not, obviously, his business to secure men whose work will remain, he wants staff that will 'go'. He will select for his permanent favours men who inspire him with confidence, men who have not any nonsense about them. Nonsense in this case is impracticable ideas of one kind or another.

X will drive down to an editorial office in a nice dogcart and during an interview, interrupted by frequent calls at a telephone, will fidget towards a window overlooking the street in order to call pointed attention to the fact that his horse will not stand. In that case he may demonstrate that there is not any nonsense about him, that he is not dreamily poetic, but up to date and practical. He makes, perhaps, a chance for himself, but he might have done still better by studying his market, by acquiring a knowledge of the characteristics, the tone and the scope of the journal he has designs on. The editor, on the other hand, merely wants to get at whether X will appeal to his own particular 'crowd'.

This tendency of dependence on the tastes of the great crowd is most handily demonstrable in the case of the Press; but it underlies every other industry. I happen to have followed the career of a man who is now still young and a very flourishing cabinet maker. He was the son of a widow in domestic service, Huguenot by descent,* merry, dark and handsome whilst a young boy, but not otherwise strikingly intelligent.

The master of his mother got him apprenticed to a working carpenter, and he developed what was practically a passion for fret-sawing. He rather lost his looks and his clothes were always dusted with the little particles of wood that fall away from the teeth of fret-saws. As soon as he was out of his time he set up for himself as a jobbing cabinet maker, in a small Walthamstow shop; he continued to pay serious attention to fretwork. Eventually he evolved what was practically a style: he made small hexagonal coffee tables, of the sort one sees now in the smoking divans of seaside hotels. These things had a kind of pierced screen, Oriental in inspiration, between each pair of legs and were painted a dead white. He made perhaps a dozen of these, with more than a dozen little stools, and some over-mantels and settees to match, all in white, with quasi-Moorish perforations.

About this time W saw an announcement in his trade paper: a certain large linoleum seller was giving one of his windows to bamboo furniture. W set off at once with a specimen coffee table under his arm; he managed to see the proprietor of this shop – it was in a well-frequented thoroughfare. The latter consented to 'stock' the rest of W's white things, which were ludicrously inexpensive. He arranged in his window an alcove in which a white coffee table, some white stools, and a white settee stood, or supported cheap Oriental trays and vases full of peacock's feathers. There was not a day to wait for the things to 'take on'.

In a few days W was turning out scores of white tables and overmantels. His ingenuity ended by no means at quasi-oriental nick-nacks, he had in him an astonishing faculty for knowing

what the public – in this case mostly young marrying couples –
could be induced to 'want'. He turned out cheap Chippendales,
cheap Louis XIVs, cheap farm-house styles; he went with his
customer, the former linoleum seller, to Arts and Crafts*
Exhibition. Whatever there appeared to them as a 'line' in
tables, chairs, beds or whatnots he could modify very slightly,
cheapen very substantially, and turn out in large quantities, and
W is rapidly growing rich.

   This, of course, is a *Roman d'un Jeune Homme Pauvre*,* but
it is something more because it casts a strong light upon the
characteristics of work in modern London. For of the worker
nowadays there is demanded more than the old-fashioned
attention to work. Unless you wish to live for posterity you
cannot any more put out good work, work that is solid and
lasting, leaving it alone to push its way in the world and to bring
you customers paying a goodly price. You must obviously
produce work that is good in the sense of being attractive for
the moment; that is the one essential. But also, as I have said,
you must have temperament – the temperament that brings
luck, because it makes you take the right step instinctively and
at the right moment. And you must have that sympathy with
the humanity around you that will let you know just what
modification of your product will for the time hold the sympathy
of the crowd. This essential holds as good for the company
promoter as for the cabinet maker. And you must have the
qualities of inspiring confidence and of knowing instinctively
whom you can trust.

   This personal element tends to become, paradoxically perhaps, of more and more importance as the spirit of combinations
spreads. And it is spreading into the most personal of the
industries of today. There died in March of 1903 a sufficiently
remarkable woman, a Mrs Russell of Southwark. She was
shrewd and eccentric, she had a passion for displaying her
fingers in an armour of gold rings, and her breast in a mail of
gold chains, and it was a certain fortune for a costermonger to
get on her soft side. For she had achieved nothing less than a
'combine' of coster barrows in Southwark.

   The tendency in all things is either towards the trustification
of all activities or towards State and Municipal trading.*[1] Into

---

[1] I do not wish to imply that the prospect pleases or displeases me. But the

either the personal factor must enter very largely. We may suppose the grocery trade to be taken over by the State. There will be no scope at all for individual brilliancy; counter clerks will take orders with about the same capabilities, and what 'rises' there may be will go either by routine or by the recommendations of foremen. These latter, as today they do, will recommend juniors who appeal to them for one reason or another. The same thing will happen if the grocery trade in the alternative becomes one vast Trust.

This tendency is as observable in a London bank as in a London cement factory. The bank manager watches and considers the personal characteristics of his clerks with an anxious solicitude. He notes the particulars of his clerk's dress and the details of his home life. A subordinate, who hopes for promotion must be careful never to be seen wheeling a perambulator for his wife; it would, if he happened to become manager of a suburban branch, damage the standing of the Bank in the eyes of the customers, excellent accountant though he may be. On

---

strong feeling against say Municipal Trading must disappear as soon as Trusts become universal. The Trusts may simply become the State as is the tendency in America. Or in the more likely alternative they may grow so oppressive that an outcry for State Trading will arise. In either case the individual trader will have disappeared, and with him the opposition to State Trading. The individual's sons and daughters will be simply the employees of the Trusts, and will view with indifference or with more probable favour their absorption by the State or the City in which they are interested. The third issue, the triumph of the co-operative system, will be so precisely the same in its effects on the individual worker that it may for my purposes be classed with either.

The broad fact remains that the individual worker for the time being is doomed. He has been so for a long time, in London at least. This again is most strikingly observable in the periodical press. Upon the whole that of literature makes of all the pursuits the most call for individuality. Yet ever since Cave* let Johnson dine behind his screen, ever since those two started the 'Gentleman's Magazine' it has become more and more essential to men of letters to live in London. And today it is impossible for the many of them to exist, or for the very few to grow rich without the aid of journalism in one or other of its manifestations. This means their becoming the employees of small or of very large combines. All the learned professions have for centuries now been combined with their headquarters in London. They have been empowered with charters to become administrative, examining, or penal bodies, of solicitors, barristers, surgeons, doctors and even pharmacists, – to become close corporations.

the other hand he must be an excellent accountant, and he must impress his superior with his knowledge of human nature. He must be able to gauge, both with his intuition and by the skilful utilisation of local gossip, what customers it is safe to trust with those overdrafts that are the life of suburban trade.

It is very much the same in cement or kindred works. A hand must commence by being a good and an industrious workman, but he must also, if he is to rise, give the impression of being very much alive and very much interested in his work. I am thinking of a case in point in some rather small works of the sort. Here there is a managing foreman whom I will call Stanley. He is perhaps twenty-nine. These works were started to work a new process about twelve years ago, and Stanley, at the time a boy, helped in making the bed of the first engine. He was particularly alert, and entered into the spirit of the thing. This at the time was not very obvious, the engine being set down on the slope of a green hill into which it has since tunnelled and cut until an arena of sand, of rubble and of chalk, opens an immense face to the lower Thames. It shelters alike on its flat surface a huge cement factory, sand works, and a large brickfield. Immense chimney shafts like thin pencils pierce up into the lower clouds; the ground is sticky and white under foot, channelled with open conduits of hot water, a maze of small lines on which run tiny locomotives, a maze of the little black shelters that cover drying bricks.

In the midst of these gray and monstrous apparitions, in the faint and sickly odour of steam, under the drops that condense and fall from the eaves of engine sheds, clambering through small holes, dressed in dull clothes, clean shaven and with sparkling eyes, Stanley moves like a spirit of romance. If he chances upon a visitor he becomes almost a spirit in ecstasy. He slaps the bed of the engine that he helped to set there, he bids workmen run the wet sand through trap doors, he explains how these three industries, set there together in that hollow, work one into another so that nothing is lost. The hot water from the boilers of the cement works runs in those open conduits to separate in the sand works the sand from the loam; the separated loam makes the bricks in the brick works. He waves his hands and shouts in the immense roar of pebble-crushing machines to explain how what appears to be a lot of old ploughshares tied together with rope is really a nice device of his own for regulating the pressure on the crushing rollers. These things are the great, the romantic facts of his world. Because they are so, his managing director has advanced him very quickly from being a shovel boy, paddling in the warm and sandy water, to be superintendent of the whole works.

But it is almost more important that the hands all like him. His director can go home and sleep, or leave the place for days on end, confident that Stanley has the knack of infusing into his men some of his own interest in the work itself, and that he will not by petty tyrannies bring on a strike. That particular human quality, the particular sort of artistic delight in his work which brings to birth an *esprit de corps*, is almost the most precious quality that a man can offer in these days of organisation. Without at least a share of it Stanley could never have risen from the ranks; with as much as he has there is no limit to his possibilities.

At the same time, as a defect of this particular quality of work in London, the making of Stanley has meant throwing out of work of a whole small industry. It has caused to disappear almost the last of the old small flotillas of barges that used to dredge sand by hand from the bottom of the river. (Thames sand is indispensable in the London building trade; it is stipulated for in all the contracts for honest mortar.)

Travelling through all that eastern London of toil, no thought is more oppressive than that: a little way away or at a great distance people are unceasingly working to mature new processes that will ruin any one of the works that the eye rests on. Nothing can well be more tragic than such an announcement as this, which one may read any day in a trade paper: 'Owing to the competition of the new D— process of Messrs W—, the D— Co of Plumstead have been forced to close that branch of their works. Two thousand workmen have been discharged this week. Messrs T—, of Erith, have notified their ability to take over fifty mechanics at once and fifty-nine more later on. If other firms requiring men will communicate with the secretary of the D— workers' Union they will assist in mitigating the local distress.'

I must confess to finding that thought the most exciting and the most sinister that can come into one's head in those parts of the vast city. They are grim, they are overhung with perpetual miasma, they lie low in damp marshes. Square and stumpy chimneys rise everywhere in clusters like the columns of ruined temples overhung with smirchings of vapour. Great fields are covered with scraps of rusty iron and heaps of fluttering rags; dismal pools of water reflect on black waste grounds the dim skies. But all these things, if one is in the mood, one may find stimulating, because they tell of human toil, of human endeavour towards some end with some ideal at that end. But the other thing is sinister, since the other influences are working invisible, like malign and conscious fates, below the horizon.

To assist at the obsequies of one of these great works is more suggestive than to have seen the corpses in the snow of the retreat from Moscow.* It is more horrible because the sufferers have fought in a fight much more blind and suffer inarticulately in the midst of their suffering children and in the face of their desolate homes. They suffer for no apparent principle, for no faith, for no fame, for no nation, for no glory; they suffer the shame of poverty without the compensating glory of defeat. They have not ever seen their Napoleon ride slowly along their cheering lines.

For London, if it attracts men from a distance with a glamour like that of a great and green gaming table, shows, when they are close to it, the indecipherable face of a desperate battle field, without ranks, without order, without pity and with very little of discoverable purpose. Yet those that it has attracted it holds for ever, because in its want of logic it is so very human.

CHAPTER 4

London at Leisure

I was talking some time ago to a timekeeper in one of the bus yards in the west of London. In a sort of very clean square of stables horses stood patiently in couples with their traces hooked over their backs, the chains jingling a little, and yardmen with their braces about their loins bent over pails of water into which they stirred a powder of coarse oatmeal. A big man in painfully clean-washed corduroys came furtively and hesitatingly under the square entrance arch. His eyes wandered round, resting with a look of acquaintance and friendship upon the small litters of straw that lay outside each of the house doors. He began fumbling in an inner pocket painfully for his testimonials, his 'character'. The timekeeper said, 'No, mate, no job here', and the man, after staring again at the straw, turned away without a word spoken, painfully shy, tired, and mutely disappointed, slowly as if he had all the time of the world upon his hands. They had had five men like him already in the yard that same morning.

This particular man appealed to me – and upon the whole you cannot hope to find in London anything much more pathetic, in a small way, than the peculiar 'action' of a genuine labourer seeking work, his slow and heavy movements, his vacant and undecided air, his evident not knowing what to do with his hands, and all the signs that go to tell of a hungry and undesired leisure, and the fact that, as a rule, you cannot do anything in the world really to help him. This man was one of a great many employees in a soap factory that the vagaries of one of our Napoleons of Finance had lately caused to 'shut down'. It was a hopeless bankruptcy at a time when trade was too slow to make it feasible for the debenture-holders to carry on the work. All the hands had been thrown as if out of a barrow to find other holes somewhere in London. This man had been for a fortnight without a job, and he said it seemed precious likely he wouldn't get one for a good bit.

He had walked that morning from East Ham way right across to Hammersmith but his case was not a particularly poignant one. He had a missis but no kids, and his missis did a bit of charing for a Mrs North and a Mrs Williamson. He had been, as a boy, a wagoner's mate – one of those boys who walk with a brass-bound whip beside a team either in the cart or in the plough – in Lincolnshire. But things had seemed a bit slow down there and he had come up to London to find shorter hours, lighter jobs, better pay, and the chance to save a bit – to find, in fact, these streets paved with gold.

'Mart's well be back there,' he said, with a humorous smile, as if the idea were absurd. For London, if its work, even from the outside, have the mysterious and magnetic attraction of an immense gambling table, may, and inevitably does, rob those it attracts of that tremulous and romantic idea. The gambling becomes a hard and almost unceasing struggle, with the pay proportionately worse, with the hours really longer because the work is so much more strenuous. But London itself and for itself takes a hold of the hearts of men; along with disillusionments grows up a hunger, like a new sense, for London only. These men in the mass never go back. When I offered to this particular man to write to a farmer who I knew was in want of a hand he looked at me as if I must be joking. He groped in his mind for a reason. 'The missis would never *hear* of it,' he said. 'Besides – ' His power of invention seemed to break down till he got out: 'Oh, London's the place!' His eyes roved along the sides of a cab that was passing and up the front of an establishment called, I think, the West London Stores. 'London's the place,' he repeated. I objected that he could not see much of London inside a soap factory. He considered for a moment and said: 'No, but it's the Saturday afternoons and Sundays.' He paused. 'It's when ye have your leisure.' He continued with the air of one trying to explain something difficult to a stupid person or a child: 'It's the dinner hour with your mates and the snacks of talk between whiles loading barrows. Don't you see?' He paused again for a long time and then added: 'London's the place.' He could not think of going back.

Thus what London attracts with the mirage of its work shining across the counties and the countries, London holds with the glamour of its leisure. We never go back, never really and absolutely: London for those who have once, for however short a space, been Londoners, is always on the cards, is always just beyond the horizon. We may 'go back' to the country for our health's sake, for our children's health's sake, if we can. We may 'go back' in a sense to the Colonies because we are not fitted for life or for work in London. But all the time London is calling; it calls in the middle of our work, it calls at odd moments like the fever of spring that stirs each year in the blood. It seems to offer romantically, not streets paved with gold but streets filled with leisure, streets where we shall saunter, things for the eye to rest on in a gray and glamorous light, books to read, men to be idle with, women to love.

If the idea of the 'working classes' seems to call up a picture of the black plains of the East End, the picture when the 'leisured classes' are in consideration is that of a circumscribed parallelogram of rows of tall buildings. It is a square block like a fortress that we all, more or less, are besieging – the little plot of ground bounded on the south by Piccadilly, on the west by the railings of Hyde Park, on the north by Oxford Street and on the east by Bond Street. It stands fairly well for where we should all live if we were 'really rich', it represents, as far as London is concerned, our castles in the air whether we should be contented with a small, bright house in one of the angles of Mayfair, with a suite of rooms in the P—* that overlooks the Green Park, or whether we should be contented with nothing less than one of the palaces in Park Lane.

These streets are quiet, for London, and bright and well swept and almost joyous. From their exclusiveness one steps out so easily into Rotten Row, which stands for the high-water mark of out-of-doors laziness in the modern world; and, if the clubs from which, as from an opera-box, one looks out across the parks towards Buckingham Palace – if those clubs are not, for social traditions, for standing, for gravity, or for place, 'in it' with the older clubs near Pall Mall or about Whitehall, they are at least more pagan in the sense of being more humanly enjoyable to the uninitiated. A man can, in these places, lounge so utterly and entirely.

And that, in essentials, is the charm of social life in London. There are not any really rigid barriers; one has so immense a choice within the limits of any purse. There are in London institutions that are rigidly exclusive, but these are so rare as to be merely the spice of the large dish. This, of course, is only the case comparatively with the other capitals of the world.

It is, for instance, impossible for a French outsider to 'get into' the real society of the Faubourg St Germain; a relatively great number of quarterings* are needed, a certain tradition, a certain habit of mind, a certain, let us say, inanity. It is also relatively impossible in Berlin to 'get into' the military, or the blood aristocracies. Money cannot do it, or personal charm, or imnmense talents. It is absolutely impossible in Vienna where society is ruled by a Court, and that Court absolutely insists on quarterings as a social qualification. It is, I should say, with certain modifications the same in St Petersburg and in Rome. It is almost more markedly so in Madrid and Lisbon. In all these places a man is 'placed'; he knows his place and it is known for him.

But in London, comparatively speaking, a man stands pretty well by what he is or by what he has. He cannot, or course, occupy the throne but, given the temperament or the wealth he can sit in almost any other chair. Essentially, the other capitals ask a man to be something; London society asks him to give something – whether dinners or personal charm, whether financial tips or a soothing personal effacement.

It is probably this last characteristic that is the most essential, or, at least, the most attainable. It is that that, as it were, gives every man his chance. Paradoxically enough the reason for it is that London society is made up of such intensely individual types that the comparatively characterless man is absolutely essential. He fills up holes, he tones down dinner parties, he may be relied on not to jar, not to shine – not to worry one's nerves. In a society which is made up very much of strong individualities more or less constantly at war, self-effacement has a charm; the listener grows very precious.

And, upon the whole, in the other capitals of the world the thing is very exactly the other way round. In societies where the essential quality is birth, individuals are rare. In those closed ranks men are very much alike, and women – in character, in point of view, in gesture, in speech. In consequence an individuality tells. It is not, as in London, questioned, doubted and mistrusted; it is, if the individual belongs to the society, welcomed as a rather pleasant relief from the dead level.

The fascination of life in London is essentially its freedom. In society of the one type you may do very much what you like short of eating peas with a knife, wearing a felt hat with a frock coat, or a coloured tie with evening dress. You may, in the realm of ideas, be as heterodox as you please; you may 'pass' being a Roman Catholic, a Buddhist, even a Jew or Mohammedan. (Obviously it is not good form to intrude your personal views in mixed company, but you are allowed your freedom of private thought.) But in, say, Catholic circles in France, entry is barred to a man suspected of being a Protestant or a Republican.

But if, on the one hand, private freedom of views is permissible in London, the rule that you must not express in Society any views at all is so rigid, that any infringement of it causes a shudder. It is a want of tact. Examined into minutely, you will find again, as the basis of this characteristic, the individual unit. There is not any London type. London is a meeting place of all sorts of incongruous types, and, if you must not utter your views, it is simply because you run so sure a risk of hurting the feelings of every individual near you. In Catholic circles abroad you may talk freely of the Deity, the Virgin, the Saviour, or the Saints, because what is thought about these divinities is rigidly defined. In London society you may be — it is considered commendable to be — devout in private, but it is a shuddering offence to mention the Deity in company. Similarly all metaphysical topics, all political matters going below the surface or likely to cause heat, the consideration of sexual questions, the mention of the poor or the suffering, are avoided. This is, in origin, because your neighbour at dinner has his or her private views, and has a right to them. You do not enquire into them, you do not know them, and you cannot air your own views because they will probably give offence.

The net result is to make London conversations singularly colourless; but they become singularly unexhausting. No call is made upon your brain or your individuality; it is precisely not 'good form' to make any kind of display. You may be yourself as much as you please, but it must be yourself in a state of quiescence. No strain at all is put upon you, because it is the height of good manners to have no manners at all.

This of course is most noticeable abroad, where the Londoner is celebrated for his atrociously bad manners. He does not bow over his hat on entering a room; he sits down on any chair, he has no gesticulations of pleasure, he stops short at being well

groomed and undemonstrative. There is not, in fact, any etiquette in London, there is only a general rule against obtruding
your personality – a general rule against animation in society.
'Die verstaendigste und geistreichste aller europaeischen Nati-
onen hat sogar die Regel, 'never interrupt', das elfte Gebot
genannt,' says Schopenhauer.*[1] But obviously if you never
interrupt you must have schooled yourself to care little for the
discussion you have in hand, or you must avoid the discussion
of subjects you care for.

Essentially we may say that the other great societies of Europe
prescribe rigid codes of manners, and a member of society
attains to self-respect by his knowledge of these codes. He tries
in fact to do something. London society has no code, it
prescribes an attitude of mind. You do not enter a London
drawing-room with one, three or six bows; you do not kiss your
hostess's hand. But you lounge in and get through that ceremonial contact as best suits you. You try to show no impressment at
all. For it may be said that, in London, the mark of the leisured
class is to be without restraint. One may go even further: to be
conscious of any restraint is to be guilty of bad manners.

For supposing a severe moralist frown, at a dinner, because
the guests, being all intimate, calling each other by familiar
nicknames, sit unbracing genially, ladies and all, with their feet
on the table. The frown will – and, after all, quite rightly – be
set down as a piece of 'unsoundness'. For, in the first place,
what does a moralist – a man with an occupation or a mission
– seek in this particular galley? It is – this particular leisured
class – circumscribed and walled in; it circumscribes itself, too.
It is, as it were, a deer park within London; a Zoological
Gardens within the ring of a Regent's park.

If we may call the very poor – the sweated workers – a *caput
mortuum* of the body politic, beyond hope of being raised,
beyond hope of being moralized upon because they are always
at work: so, in the London of Leisure we may call this other
class above hope of being touched, above hope of being moral-
ised upon – because they are always at leisure. It is unprofitable
for the moralists to worry about them: they have reverted to

---

[1] 'The most understanding and most spiritual of all the European nations
(the English) has named the rule 'never interrupt', the eleventh commandment.'
– *Parerga und Paralipomena*. 'Über Lärm und Geräusch', p. 679.

savagery, really. Having no work they must needs disport themselves – and the occupation of the idle must necessarily tend towards display. Emulation in display tends, humanity being poor humanity, towards barbarism. (Not towards primitive barbarism, be it said, for that devotes all its energies towards the straitening of its tribal laws, of its moral and ceremonial observances. It veils its women; prescribes fasts; enjoins hygienic ablutions, abstinence from certain meats, usuries, fornications, and the depicting of actual objects.)

But this other barbarism, which comes after a race, a Society, or a family, has passed upwards through the painful strata of observances and of tribal laws, is a breaking of all bonds. It is humanity drawing a deep breath, 'going fanti',* running amuck through the laws of public opinion. It is the man that is in all of us breaking loose and seeking to wallow. It may not go further than putting our feet on the dining table. than pouring champagne cup upon our host's head, or, as an amiable bishop put it the other day, ' neighing after our neighbours' wives', but, having arrived at that stage, these 'sets' begin again to evolve their tribal laws, so that not to put up our feet, not to pour champagne cup, or not to 'neigh' is to be an enemy to that particular republic. This phenomenon does not matter, it is past banning and past curing. You cannot learn any moral lesson from a Malay running amuck – and, as the Chinese proverb has it, 'It would be hypocrisy to seek for the person of the Sacred Emperor in a low tea house.' Thus it is really much better for the moralist not to think about them. If, in the guise of a Savonarola,* he fill them with fear for their immortal souls, it will not mean any more than a hysterical revival. In the body politic they do not 'count', they are a shade more hopeless than the very poor, they will run their course towards ruin, physical decay, or towards that period of life when ginger being no longer hot in a mouth that has lost all savours, they will become aged devotees and perhaps make for edification.

No doubt to the passionate reformer, of whatever code, the idea of so many individuals living the life of beasts is horribly disturbing. (I know, indeed, one reformer who was driven to fits of rage at the waste of time in a family of the leisured class. They had lived at this particular reformer's house in the country, and apparently washed themselves ten times a day.) But no doubt, too, this phenomenon makes for good to the body politic.

Work is the original curse of mankind because it is the original medicine. We may go on working till we drop, occupying our minds, keeping our bodies sound – but the moment we drop work our minds decay, our bodies atrophy, it is all over with us in this world. As with individuals so with the Body Politic, or with London, the modern World Town.

Whilst, in essentials, it is a Town of Work it keeps all on going; it sweats out at the top these atrophied individuals, or it sweats them out at the bottom (they hang around the street posts and make books outside the doors of public houses); and thus Work, the medicine, purges the unhealthy corpuscles of the blood or revenges itself of the too healthy. For if we may call the poor loafer the unhealthy, we must call the rich leisured class the too healthy. In one way or another their ancestors, their family, their *gens*, have worked too much for them: they are left without the need to labour. If, then, these families, these 'sets', could preserve a stolid middle course, if they could live for ever within their incomes, restrict their families, and remain leisured for ever, the end of London would indeed be near. But human nature steps in.

So whilst there is emulation there is hope. We shall, it is to be trusted, go on, 'cutting dashes' until we drop out, until our children sink down to rise up again fighting, or until we die out, childless and forgotten, unhealthy corpuscles, purged and got rid of. There would be a greater danger to London if this Leisured Class were to spread very far; but that, for a city so vast, must mean an accumulation of wealth inconceivable, and in these latter days practically impossible. Rome decayed because, being mistress of the world, she robbed the whole world and lived profusely, rioting for centuries upon the spoils of primeval empires. But there is no such hope any longer for London; she has her too urgent competitors, and the primeval empires have been by now too often gutted to leave any very substantial pickings. So that the wealth of London has to be gained by work, and this fortress of the leisured class remains as a lure, as a sort of Islands of the Blest,* glamorous in the haze above Park Lane and Mayfair, an incentive to health because wealth means leisure; wealth means work, and work health. A nobler incentive would of course be nobler, and no doubt it might be more valuable when attained. But perhaps an all-seeing Providence arranges the world in the best way for the child that

is man, for the child that will train, harden itself, strive and race
– upon no matter what cinder track – for a prize cup that is of
no intrinsic value, for a championship that carries nothing with
it but the privilege to struggle and retain the honour, or to rest,
grow fat, and decay.

So, save for the very few whom the reformers influence, and
save for the very few whom philosophy really makes wise, and
the very few whose wings have been singed – for all the really
healthy and not selfconscious humanity of the world that is
London, this mirage of the Leisured Class, hanging above the
smoke of the roofs, appearing in the glamour of the morning
dreams, gilding how many castles, in how many airs, is the
incentive to life in London.

'It takes a good deal out of you', this leisured life of display.
You rush more or less feverishly, gathering scalps of one sort or
another; being 'seen' in the record number of places where
anyone who is anyone can be seen; you pack your days with
drives on coaches, fencing matches, luncheons, afternoons,
dressings and re-dressings, dinners, the founding of new
religions in drawing rooms, polo matches, cricket matches,
standing against walls at dances, neighing perhaps after your
friends' wives, seeking heaven knows what at operas, theatres,
music halls, dashing out into the home counties and back, or
really and sensuously enjoying the music of a good concert. At
any rate you live very full and laborious days, seeking excitements – until finally excitement leaves you altogether. If you are
really in luck, if you are really someone, each of these events of
your day is 'something'. Each concert is something portentous
and, in the world of music perhaps, makes history. Each religion
that you see founded is to the sociologist something really
significant, each cricket match a real 'event' in which the best
muscle and the best brain of the day is striving, delivering
beautiful balls and making deft and beautiful strokes. But each
of these things sinks back into the mere background of your
you. You are, on the relentless current of your life, whirled past
them as, in a train, you are whirled past a succession of beautiful
landscapes. You have 'seen' such and such a social event as you
have seen, say, Damascus, from a saloon window.

You carry away from it a vague kaleidoscope picture – lights
in clusters, the bare shoulders of women, white flannel on green
turf in the sunlight, darkened drawing rooms with nasal voices

chanting parodies of prayers, the up and down strokes of fiddle bows, the flicker of fifty couples whirling round before you as with a touch of headache you stood in a doorway, a vague recollection of a brilliant anecdote, the fag end of a conversation beneath the palms of a dimmed conservatory, and a fatigue and a feverish idea that if you had missed any one of these unimportant things you would have missed life.

But, if you had been a beanfeaster* who missed a beanfeast, or if you had been a Saturday footballer who missed one match, you might have missed so much more of your life. And, indeed, since life is no more than a bundle of memories, your life is so much shorter, since you remember seasons, not events. It is with you: 'The season when good old Hinds had his place in Cadogan Square;' or, 'The year, don't you remember? when we used to drink barley water', or, 'Hermit's year'. But the Saturday footballer remembers so many glorious Saturdays relieved by so many blank weeks. He remembers the splendid crowded journeys back – 'The time when Old Tommy sang "Soldiers of the Queen"' – 'The time when we had the cask of beer on the luggage rack coming back from playing Barnes' – 'The time when Black and Moses stuck the ticket collector under the seat and kept him there till Waterloo.'

So the life of seasons and years is shorter, swifter, more regretful, less filled. And, the breaks being less marked, the life itself is the more laborious and less of a life. For it is in the breaks, in the marking time, that the course of a life becomes visible and sensible. You realise it only in leisures within that laborious leisure; you realise it, in fact, best when, with your hands deep in your trousers pockets, or listless on your watch-chain, you stand, unthinking, speculating on nothing, looking down on the unceasing, hushed, and constantly changing defile of traffic below your club windows. The vaguest thoughts flit through your brain: the knot on a whip, the cockade on a coachman's hat, the sprawl of a large woman in a victoria, the windshield in front of an automobile. You live only with your eyes, and they lull you. So Time becomes manifest like a slow pulse, the world stands still; a four-wheeler takes as it were two years to crawl from one lamp-post to another, and the rustle of newspapers behind your back in the dark recesses of the room might be a tide chafing upon the pebbles. That is your deep and blessed leisure: the pause in the beat of the clock that comes now and then to make life seem worth going on with. Without that there would be an end of us.

For, whether we are of the leisured class, whether we are laundry-women, agricultural labourers, dock labourers, or bank clerks, it is that third state that makes us live. Brahmins* would call it contemplation; the French might use the word, *assoupisse-ment.** It would be incorrect to call it reverie since it is merely a suspension of the intellectual faculties; it is a bathing in the visible world: it is a third state between work and amusement – perhaps it is the real Leisure.

It is not obviously a product of London alone. For your agricultural labourer who hangs over a gate at dusk, just gently swinging a foot and gazing, wrapt unthinking and voluptuous, at black and white, at speckled, at bright red and flame-plumaged poultry on the green below him, tastes it very well along with the flavour of the straw in his mouth – and the women who, after their hard days, stand above the half doors of cottages and gaze at nothing. But with them it is not a third state, since it takes the place of amusement as well as rest. Your London dock labourer really has this third state, since along with his hard physical work he has his sing-songs, his club nights, his visits to music halls, his nights when he takes his 'missus' to the theatre. I knew one very good fellow, a plasterer's labourer, hardworking, making good money, and as regular as a church clock. His hobby was chaffinches. In the mornings before work and in the evenings he gave a certain amount of time to teaching his birds to pipe. At nightfalls he would go to his public house for a couple of pints of ale and a few pipes. On a Saturday afternoon he was shaved and went to a club where there were singing and debates. He always came home sober enough to put beside his bed – he was a bachelor – a pailful of treacle beer that he had brewed himself, and an indiarubber tube.

And there on a Sunday he would lie nearly through the day sucking up the treacle beer through the tube and gazing at the ceiling, thinking nothing at all, letting his eyes follow the cracks in the plaster from one wall to another, backward and forward for ever. Late in the afternoon he would get up, dress himself carefully in his best; wrap his chaffinch cages in old handker-chiefs, and, carrying them, saunter along Petticoat Lane, look restfully at the cages of birds exposed for sale, meditating a purchase for next year, passing the time of day with a Jew or two, and losing himself, stolid, quiet, and observant, in the thick crowd. He would come to a greengrocer's shop, the door open, the interior a black and odorous darkness, where you trod upon cabbage leaves and orange paper. Behind this was another dark room, in the centre of which a ladder stood up going into an upper loft through a trap-door. This loft was the 'Cave of Harmony' where, in the light of brilliant gas jets were held the contests of the piping chaffinches. There, taking the gas jets for a fiercer sun, the little birds sang shrilly and furiously one against another, the attentive crowd of faces around them, thrown into deep shadows and strong lights, hard featured and intense, with every eye fixed upon the small and straining singer, fingers ticking off turns in the song and a silence broken by no shuffling of feet and no clearing of throats.

So, having scored his 'marks', our friend would go slowly and soberly home; set another pailful of treacle beer to brew against next Sunday morning, and put himself quietly to bed.

Thus his life was perfectly regular and calm; hard muscular work giving place to sober amusement, dashed once a week with that intense leisure of lying still, looking at the ceiling and thinking nothing. On off days, bank holidays and the like, he would take his cages, wrapped up, under his arm, out into Epping Forest. For these chaffinch fanciers have a notion – no doubt it is a true one – that unless their captive birds refresh their memory of the wild song by chanting against free chaffinches in the woods or parks, they will lose the brilliance of their note, and finally mope and die. There are in London many thousands of men like this.

Chaffinches, bullfinches, prize bantams, prize rabbits, whippets, bull terriers, canaries, and even pigs occupy their leisure moments, and are regarded with pride by their wives, and awe by their young children. These breeders and fanciers are mostly country born, deliberate, gentle, sober, with a pipe generally in the corner of the mouth, from which come rare jets of smoke accompanying words as rare and as slow. And their 'fancies' provide them with that companionship of animals that is such a necessity to the country-bred Englishman. It gives them a chance to get rid of some of the stores of tenderness towards small living things which, for lack of words, they cannot so well lavish on their wives and children. I have known a carter who did not apparently trouble himself in the least about illnesses in his own house, driven to a state of distraction because one of his old companions, a draught-horse, was on the point of death.

They give him, too, these 'fancyings', not only the chance to gaze ineffably, like the agricultural labourer, at the motions of animals, but the chance of emulation, the chance, if you will, of sharing in a sport. That, as it were, is what London supplies, and what makes London in a way both attractive and salutary. For we may say that the man who ceases to compete ceases to be a perfect man, and, in the actual stages of heavy manual work there is no room for emulation. It is true that in the country you have ploughing matches, but they touch only the very few; you have cottage garden prizes, but those are artificially fostered 'from above', and, indeed, they call for efforts too like those of the everyday work to afford much of an occupation for a man's leisure. – So that, as a rule, these prizes flourish most in the neighbourhood of the small towns, and fall to railway signalmen, cobblers and the non-agricultural. Starling and sparrow shoots are, of course, mere bank holiday carouses, not the hobbies that are necessary for the everyday life of a man. Thus the country districts are depleted.

And, inasmuch as the arts are matters of association, we, loving a picture, a melody, a verse, because for obscure reasons it calls up in us forgotten memories of times when we were young, in love or happy, so these 'fancies' which are Arts, call up in the hearts of these countrymen become town-labourers, moods like those they felt in forgotten green fields. I know a man who breeds pheasants in the green enclosure of a City churchyard, and when, towards October in the early black mornings of that tiny and shut-in square, roofed in from the sky by plane leaves high up near the steeple, overlooked by the gleaming plate-glass windows of merchants' offices, these noble birds utter their shrill, prolonged and wild crockettings, like peals of defiant laughter, their owner says rhapsodically: 'Doesn't it make you think of Norfolk?' It makes me think of covert rides in Kent, dripping with dew, and of the clack of the beaters' sticks and their shrill cries; but all the same it makes that City caretaker have all the sensuous delight of the green fields of his youth.

Nevertheless, he comments; 'It's better here nor there. – Down there it meant forty shillings if the keeper caught you so much as smelling a pheasant's neck feather.' – Here he needed no gun license, and they paid him ten times over for their keep, and kept his hands nicely full.

So the birds with their delicate gait, high and dainty spurred steps, and peering, brilliant necks, seek unceasingly for issues from the closed railings of the churchyard, and contribute all that, in London, is needed to keep their owner there for ever. I knew a Rye fisherman, a lazy, humorous scoundrel, who never went to sea when he had the price of a pint in his pocket. He grew tired of that life and became a door-keeper in some Southwark chemical works. He spends his leisure time with his hands in his pockets, leaning over the river wall, spitting into the eddies of the water and commenting on the ineptitude of the men on the dumb barges. Their sweeps dip up and down, to all appearances senselessly and futilely, and H— comments that ne'er a one of them ever seems to know that twenty yards in shore there's a current that would take them down three miles an hour faster. H— will scull you down to Greenwich for a pipe of tobacco just for the fun of the thing; whereas five shillings, in the old days, would not have induced him to scull you down from Rye to the harbour mouth, a matter of two miles. Sails, he used to say, were his business, oars being against nature. – But London has changed that, making of former toils present leisure.

Your London bus-driver takes his days off sitting on the front seat of an omnibus with his head close to that of the driver at work, just as the sailor lounges round harbours, glances along ropes with quietened but still professional eyes. – He gets in this way the feeling of leisure 'rubbed in' and, without anxieties, his mind is kept employed by the things he best understands. And it is because in London there are so many things to see, so many anecdotes to be retailed, such a constant passing of material and human objects, that London holds us.

I do not know that it really sharpens our wits: I fancy that it merely gives us more accidental matters on which to display them, more occurrences to which to attach morals that have been for years crystallised in our minds. – I was listening to the observations of two such bus drivers. They were like this: of a red-nosed fourwheel driver: 'Now then old danger signal!' To a driver of a very magnificent state carriage: 'Where are you going with that glass hearse?' Of a very small man conducting a very

tall lady across the road: 'I reckon he wants a step ladder when
he kisses her goodnight!'

Whereupon the driver who hadn't made the remark muttered:
'Just what I was going to say, Bill. You took the very words out
of my mouth.' – Thus these famous witticisms of the London
streets are largely traditional and common property. No doubt
London breeds a certain cast of mind by applying men's
thoughts to a similar class of occurrences, but the actual
comments float in the air in class and class. In the classes that
are as a rule recruited from the country, the type of mind is
slower, more given to generalisation, less topical, more idealis-
ing. It is broader, in fact, because it has two experiences of life,
and depends less upon the daily papers.

The children of these countrymen are quite different. The
power of generalisation has left them altogether, with their town
breeding; their conversation is a collection of town topics, their
allusions are gathered from the interests of daily papers, they
have international nicknames for the food in cheap eating houses
and for common objects. – Thus whiskers become 'Krugers';
slices of German sausage are 'Kaiser's telegrams'; macaroni is
called 'A. J. B.'* out of a fancied resemblance to the entwined
legs of the Prime Minister of a certain epoch. Thus for the
Londoner the 'facts' of the daily and weekly press take the place
of any broad generalisations upon life.

It takes, too, for at least the poorer classes, the place of animal
'fancies'; it dictates, the daily and weekly press, their very
hobbies. For to a man with an individuality – and the country-
man has a strong and knotted one as a rule – his hobby is his
mental anodyne. To the real Londoner the press is that. You get
the distinction strongly in this way. My Lincolnshire waggoner
become a soapmaker's hand, has his bit of cold steak wrapped
up in a fragment of newspaper six weeks old. At lunch time he
spells out from this, laboriously, a report of the trial of a
solicitor for embezzeling £40,000. He says slowly: 'Well, well:
why *do* the Law always breed rogues and ruin fools?' – a general
speculation. He reads the report of a wife unfaithful to her
husband who has been fighting in South Africa, and he says:
'You can't trust a woman out of your sight . . . Reckon he didn't
beat her oft enow . . . A spaniel, a woman, and a walnut tree,
the ofter you beat 'em the faithfuller they be' – and many more
speculations of a general kind.

But his son, an office boy, his overseer, a smart London born workman, the clerks in his office, his general manager, the directors of the Company he serves; these sit morning after morning in their city-going trains, with the sheets held up before them, swallowing 'news' as they swallow quick lunches later on. These things pass through their quiescent minds as under the eyes of the clubman that string of vehicles: 'The Play that Failed; A Chat with the Manager' – 'Varieties in Weather' – 'Scorned Woman's Vengeance' – ' "Objected to Fireguards" ' – 'Comedy in the County Court' – 'Slavery to Drugs; Alarming Growth of the Opium Habit' – 'Country's Loneliness; Mental Isolation of the Cultured' – 'Infant Motorists; The Automobile as an Adjunct to the Nursery' – 'Home Rule for Egypt; Khedive's interest* in an Organised Agitation' – 'Married to a Scoundrel' – 'Batch of Stabbing Cases'. All these things flicker through the dazed and quiescent minds without leaving a trace, forgotten as soon as the first step is made upon the platform at Mark Lane* or the Mansion House Stations – as much forgotten as any telegraph pole that flickered past the train window out towards the suburbs. Very salient and very characteristic figures may make a certain mark upon the mind – the German Emperor is, for some reason or another, particularly impressive to the lower order of Londoner – 'Kaiser's telegrams' is an evidence of it. He will evoke some such comment as 'Willie's a bit dotty', but practically never such trite general reflections as that immense power, immense isolation, or immense conspicuousness, will drive a man to eccentricities of speech and action. And indeed, anyone who made such an observation aloud, would run the risk of being silenced with: 'Oh, don't talk like a book here.' Or: 'When we want to hear a preacher, we go to the City Temple.'* In a country cottage, on the other hand, the remark would be considered, accepted, and even commented on. This dislike for generalisations is as a rule set down as an English trait. An English trait it is not: but *the* London habit of mind it is. Probably, too, it is what has made conversation in London a lost art. It gives one something of a shock to read in Emerson: 'English stories, *bon-mots*, and table talk are as good as the best of the French. In America we are apt scholars, but have not yet attained to the same perfection: for the range of nations from which London draws, and the steep contrasts of conditions create the picturesque in society, as a broken country makes picturesque landscape, whilst our prevailing equality makes a prairie tameness: and secondly, because dressing for dinner every day at dark has a tendency to hive and produce to advantage everything good. *Much attrition has worn every sentence to a bullet.*'*

An American writing that passage today would be accused of irony, since we no longer utter sentences at dinners. Yet when we consider the ages of Johnson, of the Prince Regent, even when we think of the Table Talk of Shirley,* we must remember – and we must wonder what has become of that mighty stream. And we must wonder why we will no longer listen to talkers: why a talker is something we resent; why, in fact, a conversational artist strikes us nowadays as 'a bounder'.

The really good raconteurs of the Brummel type* did survive in London, as very old men, into the late eighties: the mild, splendid, whiskered creatures of the Crimea* still talked; the mild, splendid, and bearded creatures of the 'seventies still told anecdotes '*à propos* of' some general idea or other; nowadays we tell a 'good story' with diffidence, being afraid of being taken for a sort of Theodore Hook* or professional diner out. But, as a general rule, London limits itself to: 'Did you see that extraordinary case in the So-and-so today? . . .' or 'Have you read Such-and-such a novel? Seen such a play? Or such a picture show?' and it comments: 'Rotten, *I* think', without reason given for the condemnation.

Partly, no doubt, it is because we have become so 'democratic', as Emerson puts it, that society resents any monopolist of talk. Perhaps, too, the Englishman never did really enjoy being talked to or 'entertained'. (Indeed an American hostess has put it on record that an English guest commented to her the other day, 'But, we don't *want* to be entertained.') But, undoubtedly, conversation began to go out of fashion when the phrase: 'He speaks like a book' was first used invidiously. It marked the bifurcation of the English language: the distinction between our spoken and our written tongue. For this the periodical press must be held responsible.

London was always press-ridden. In the days of Johnson – who invented the Magazine – the Newspapers would make a prodigious fuss; they could drive a lady so sensible as Mrs Thrale-Piozzi* almost to distraction, with comments upon her debated marriage, and supply the Town with Talk – as opposed to Conversation – about such a matter as that Piozzi marriage, for days, months and years on end. And earlier, even, Defoe, who was the first of the Journalists, made Town Talk out of solid facts, unsolid fiction, or practical projects. But books still monopolised the airy realms of philosophical speculations; preachers still retained the sole right to lecture upon divinity – and books and preachers entered intimately into the lives of men and women. People read 'Clarissa' by the year, and debated, at dinner tables, as to the abstract proprieties of the case of Pamela. The Generalisation flourished; Conversation in consequence was possible.

But, with the coming of the Modern Newspaper, the Book has been deposed from its intimate position in the hearts of men. You cannot in London read a book from day to day, because you must know the news, in order to be a fit companion for your fellow Londoner. Connected thinking has become nearly impossible, because it *is* nearly impossible to find any general idea that will connect into one train of thought: 'Home Rule for Egypt', 'A Batch of Stabbing Cases', and 'Infant Motorists'. It is hardly worth while to trace the evolution of this process. In the 70s-80s the Londoner was still said to get his General Ideas from the leader writers of his favourite paper. Nowadays even the leader is dying out.

So that, in general, the Londoner has lost all power of connected conversation, and nearly all power of connected thought. But if his dinner-table has become democratized, and he will not suffer a connected talker among his friends, he still retains some liking for duly licensed preachers, some respect for the official talker or moralist. Generally speaking, he sets apart one day in seven for this individual, and, generally speaking, that one day is the Sabbath.

The stolid London of squares and clean streets, to the westward, still retains something of its Sunday morning hush: the pavements are empty, and as if whitened, and where there are the large detached houses, with bits of garden, and large old trees, the town still has its air of being a vast cemetery of large mausoleums, that no one ever visits. Then indeed that third state, the deep leisure, settles upon the middle London of the professional and merchant classes. There is a stillness, a hush. Breakfast is half-an-hour or an hour later than on other days, the perfume of coffee, the savour of bacon, of fish, of sausages, floats on a softer and stiller air. The interminable rumble of all the commissariat wagons, of butchers', of greengrocers', of stores' carts, all that unending procession that on week days rattles and reverberates throughout the morning, is stilled. In the unaccustomed quiet you can hear the decent hiss of the kettle on its tripod, you can hear the rustle of stiff petticoats coming down from the second floor, you can hear even the voices of the servants in the kitchen, just suggested, as if down there an interminable monologue were being carried on.

And beside the breakfast dishes there lie, still, the Sunday papers.* As a rule there are two of these, strips of white, and strips of buff, like supplementary table-napkins. The more venerable contain practically no news; they are glanced at to see the 'Prices' of the day before. But the arms that support these sheets are not the nervous, hurried arms of the week day; the glances meander down the columns. There is time, there is plenty of time – as if the reader in that hush and pause, realised and felt, just for once, that he is after all a creature of Eternity, with All Time before him. There is an opulence, a luxury of minutes to be bathed in, as it were, in that sort of London Sunday, that makes one understand very well why that part of London is so loth to part with its Sabbath.

The Sunday paper is now, I should say, a much more general feature than it used to be. It invades the most Sabbatarian breakfast tables. But I remember that, as a boy, I used to have to walk – in Kensington* – nearly two miles to procure an *Observer* for my father, every Sunday morning. (It was considered that the exercise was good for me, lacking my daily walk to school.) And the paper-shop was a dirty, obscure and hidden little place that during the week carried on the sale, mostly, of clandestine and objectionable broad sheets directed against the Papists. The Sunday paper, in fact, was shunned by all respectable newsagents – and, in consequence the Sunday breakfast table was a much less restful thing, since no book of sermons beside the plate could equal that respectable anodyne.

All over the town these sheets, as if they were white petals bearing oblivion, settle down, restful and beneficent, like so many doses of poppy seed. In the back-yards of small cottages, separated one from another by breast-high modern palings you find by the hundreds of thousands (it is certified by accountants) —'s Weekly News; —'s Weekly Paper; —'s News of the

Week; and, on each back doorstep, in his shirt sleeves, in his best trousers and waistcoat, voluptuously, soberly and restfully, that good fellow, the London mechanic, sits down to read the paper.

And, in general, those Sunday and Weekly Papers preach to a considerable extent. One middle class favourite contains at least six different headings under which can be found reflections on social subjects, on sporting subjects, on religious subjects, even on subjects purely jocular and on such abstruse matters as 'Are Clever Women Popular?' And the mechanics' Weeklies have sturdy 'tones' of their own; they fulminate against the vices, meannesses and hypocrisies of the wealthy; they unveil the secrets of Courts; they preach patriotism or the love of God. So that, even if he no longer go to church or chapel, the Londoner on Sunday mornings, before his Sunday dinner, gets as a rule his dose of general reflections. And it is characteristic of him that, although he cannot bear preaching that he might have to answer – conversational preaching – he dearly loves the preacher who is beyond his reach. He will listen to sermons, to funeral orations, to public speeches, to lectures; he loves no novel that has not a moral basis of one kind or another, that has not some purpose or other, that does not preach *some* sermon; upon the stage he likes most of all moralising old men and heroic generalisations in favour of one virtue or another. But it is characteristic of the strong lines that he draws between life and the arts,that although he is never tired of seeing a Hamlet upon the stage he will call a Hamlet of private life morbid, dangerous, unhealthy and insupportable.

Thus, in the London of leisure, any social intercourse between men and women is nowadays become almost impossible. For no man can be himself without sooner or later proclaiming whatever may be the particular moral that he draws from life. He could not really utter his thoughts without revealing the fact that he loves virtue, or does not; or that he considers there is such a thing as virtue, or is not. He is therefore driven, the social Londoner at his leisure, to action instead of to speech. He puts his feet on the dinner table; beguiles his after dinners with cards, with recitations, with mechanical pianos, with the theatres, with moonlight automobile drives or with watching skating competitions on artificial ice. He plays golf; he witnesses cricket matches, football matches, billiard matches; he goes to two-penny gaffs* in Mile End or parades in dense and inarticulate crowds of young men and young girls, for hours of an evening, in front of the shops of the great highways.

And these paradings are, for the million or so of the young people of this huge world that is London, the great delight, the great feature of a life otherwise featureless enough. In externals one parade is like another, but the small gradations are infinite. Thus in one parade there will be a great number of sets each of the same social level; each set with its gossip, its chaff, its manner of accost, its etiquette, its language. You get, as it were, an impression of entering one vast family party amid the rustle of feet, of dresses, the clitter-clatter of canes, the subdued shrieks of laughter, the hushed personal remarks. As a rule in all these parades, in the Fleet Street 'Monkey Walk' as at Shepherd's Bush; in Islington as in Mile End Road; the youths early in the evening stand in knots, cloth caps not consorting with bowler hats and straw-yards with neither. They talk with a certain ostentation and a certain affectation of swagger, boasting, or acting as chorus in praise of one another. The girls parade up and down arm in arm, white aprons being shunned by stuff dresses, and feather hats shunning the straws perched forward over the eyes. Heads steal round swiftly over shoulders as line of girls passes knot of youths, and at these electric moments the voices grow higher and little shoves and nudges pass like waves in a field of corn. There is not any psychical moment for pairing off, but the process begins as the kindly dusk falls. A youth slips away from a knot, a girl hangs back from a line, till little by little the knots dwindle away altogether and there are no more lines.

The ceremonials of the actual greeting are astonishingly various and more rigidly observed than the etiquette of the Court of Spain. In Westbourne Grove the young shop assistant raises his bowler, drawls 'How are you, Miss—?' for all the world as they do in Rotten Row. In the Mile End Road and in Shepherd's Bush the factory girls slap likely youths violently upon the back and are violently poked in the side for answer, both girl and young man uttering obscenities positively astounding, without any obscene intention in the world. And then commences, mysterious and ceremonial, the walking out, the period of probation, the golden age. For, after all, it is a golden age, an age of vague emotions, of words uttered, insignificant, but fraught with more meaning in each absurd syllable than in all the tirades of Romeo* to the moon: 'Do you like fringes?' 'Um! – ah! – um! – Well – .' 'There, you *are* a one – .' 'I dote on blue eyes – .'

So that, by nine o'clock, the parades are full of couples, orderly, quiet, moving unceasingly up and down, with conversation utterly exhausted, with the glamorous fall of light and shade, with titillating emotions, with inscrutable excitements, rustling, supremely alive and supremely happy, with here and there a violent heartache, and here and there a great loneliness. And here for the good democrat is the best sight – the really good sight – of London at leisure, since here is London, the great London of the future, the London that matters to the democrat, in the making. This is London really young, really pagan, really idyllic, really moral, really promising a future to the race, really holding its population by the spell that nothing will ever break, the spell of contagious humanity and of infinite human contacts. These are the Londoners who will never go back.

So by her leisure moments London holds us. And if you desire a sight, equally impressive, of London at leisure, go down Piccadilly to Hyde Park Corner on a pleasant summer day. On the right of you you have all those clubs*with all those lounging and luxuriating men. On the left there is a stretch of green park, hidden and rendered hideous by recumbent forms. They lie like corpses, or like soldiers in a stealthy attack, a great multitude of broken men and women, they, too, eternally at leisure. They lie, soles of boots to crowns of heads, just out of arms's reach one from the other for fear of being rifled by their couch-mates. They lie motionless, dun-coloured, pitiful and horrible, bathing in leisure that will never end. There, indeed, is your London at leisure; the two ends of the scale offered violently for inspection, confronting and ignoring steadily the one the other. For, in the mass, the men in the windows never look down; the men in the park never look up.

In those two opposed sights you have your London, your great tree, in its leisure, making for itself new sap and new fibre, holding aloft its vigorous leaves, shedding its decayed wood, strewing on the ground its rotten twigs and stuff for graveyards.

CHAPTER 5

Rest in London

In the black and dismal cloisters of our Valhalla – for still for London's heroes it is 'Victory or Westminster Abbey', though Nelson,* who uttered the words, is buried under all the stones of St Paul's – there is a small, pale mural tablet. 'In memory of Elizabeth, Dear Child', it reads, and sets us thinking of all sorts of dead children, dear in their day, and now how utterly unremembered, as wavelets are forgotten! And recumbent before it is a blackened paving stone, smoothed with the attrition of thousands of the feet of Londoners, of American tourists, of Members of Parliament, of prostitutes, of school boys. It states that here lie the remains of so and so many monks who died of the plague so and so many centuries ago.

When I was last in that dim place a man with a quick, agitated step hurried up and down the cloisters like a dog nosing out a rabbit in a hedge. He had a penetrating eye, a sharp nose, and high, thin cheekbones. He caught my glance and suddenly stretched out a hand. His voice was sonorous and rather pompous, with the *ore rotundo**in which Victorian poets used to read their own poems to one another. He uttered:

And I said:
Happy are they that do slumber and take their solace here
For they cease from their labours and have known the worst.*

He added, confidentially and confidently that: into this fane his corpse would be translated by his thousand votaries of the day to come. His name was one that posterity would not willingly let die.

His name was Tockson; he was by trade a cobbler, and he was rather a good poet. I really believe that Posterity might be none the worse if it ever come to read some of the verses that, with his own hands, he printed at odd moments on grocers' bag-paper and stored in the back of his shop. He troubled no reigning sovereign and no established poet with his verses; he never sent them to papers; sometimes he wrapped up repaired boots in an odd sheet, and he was not in the least discontented or in the least mad, unless it be a madness to trust in the literary judgement of Posterity and to take 'Marlowe's mighty line'*(the words were for ever on his lips) as a model.

He liked these cloisters, he said, because he could 'contemplate the memorials' of forgotten monks, legislators, children and philanthropists freezing in the cold and soot outside the walls, whilst it was his destiny to be 'translated' from Kensal Green Cemetery into the inner warmth of the 'fane'. And it pleased him to recite his verses there, because there, it seemed to him, they sounded better than in Clerkenwell.

He came to see me once or twice, then I lost touch with him, and going down to Clerkenwell, found that his little shop had another tenant. He had been run over by a brewer's dray. His verses – half a hundred-weight of them – had been removed by a medical student from the hospital to which he had been taken. There were vague ideas in Clerkenwell that they were going to be made into a book, so that Posterity may still benefit, and his dust, which duly lies in Kensal Green, may still ensue 'translation'. London is full of such men – poets, generals, framers of laws, men of great mechanical talents, of great strength of will, of lofty intellects. They get called 'characters' because they never have the chance, or have not the luck, the knack of self-advertisement, the opening to use their talents, their wills, their intellects. And this is the heaviest indictment that can be brought against a city or a world – that it finds no employment for its talents, that it uses them merely to form layers, as it were, of fallen leaves, that it blunts our sense of individualities.

This London does more than any other place in the world. As a city, it seems, as has been said, not only to turn Parsees*into Londoners but to make us, who are Londoners, absolutely indifferent to the Parsees, the Kaffirs,* the pickpockets or the men of genius we may pass in its streets. It blunts, by its vastness, their peculiarities, and our interest it dulls. So that it seems to be a City formed, not for you and me, not for single men, but for bands of Encyclopaedists, Corporations, Societies. Speaking roughly, we may say that the pleasantest size for a graveyard – and what is London but a vast graveyard of stilled hopes in which the thin gnat-swarm of the present population dances its short day above the daily growing, indisturbable detritus of all the past at rest? – the pleasantest size for a graveyard is one in which each man and woman at rest could rise up and proclaim: 'In my day I played a part. I had an influence upon the whole community here. Who is here that does not know my virtues and my vices? I planted the chestnut that gives all that shade on the green.' But imagine the great London 'Cemeteries'* – for they are graveyards no longer – those vast stretches of heavy clay land, desecrated with all manner of hideous and futile excrescences that no passer-by will be caught to look at, appealing like piteous beggars in endless rows for the charity of your glance; the trees that appear half unreal in the mistiness because they are such that no one would place anywhere but in a 'Cemetery'; the iron railings that are grotesque because they serve to keep nothing within a space that no living mortal is anxious to enter. But no doubt it is the penalty of being dead that one's memorial should be grotesque: the penalty of fighting against oblivion which is irresistible and pitiless. And, no doubt, it is with the sense of the fitness of things that London, the city of oblivion, consigns her dead to the distance of dim and grim suburbs.

At any rate, there they take their rest and grow forgotten. For it is impossible to imagine the ghost of, say, Macadam,* if Macadam be buried in a London cemetery – rising up at the end of some dreary and immense vista, and calling to its fellows: 'I made my mark in my day: I influenced you all.' That unfamiliar voice would arouse no other spirit; late comers would answer sleepily: 'Oh, our roads are all wood and asphalte now. Who are you?'

And, if that for all units be the pleasantest for our resting-places, it is also the most human of units for those still labouring on this earth. For, as soon as a city becomes a mass of Corporations, individualities die out and are wasted of necessity. We may consider Athens, which was a city not more vast than is Kensington High Street: probably its inhabitants were not really more cultured or more wise, but certainly they had, each one of them, better chances of influencing *all* their fellow inhabitants. And that for humanity would seem, in the Individualist's eyes, to be the best of social units. Only the most hardened of Democrats, seeing humanity not as poor individuals but as parts of a theory, as negligible cog-wheels of a passionless machine, would deny that, from a human point of view Athens was better than Kensington High Street, or than Westminster itself. So London casts oblivion upon her dead and clouds out the individualities of her living.

We talk of the Londoner and we firmly believe there *is* a Londoner: but there is none. If, in walking along the streets we open our eyes, if we search for him, we never meet him. We see men like Jews, men like Arviragus,* men with a touch of the negro, costermongers with the heads of Julius Caesars, but the Londoner we never see – and the search is painful. An awakened sense of observation is in London bewildering and nerve-shattering, because there are so many things to see and because these things flicker by so quickly. We drop the search very soon. And these great crowds chill out of us the spirit of altruism itself, or make of that spirit a curse to us. Living in a small community we know each member of it. We can hope to help, or to be interested in, each man and woman that we meet on the roads, or we can at least pay to each one the tribute of a dislike. But that, in London, is hopeless. The most we can do is to like or dislike bodies of men. If we read the 'Morning—' we have a contempt for the readers of the 'Daily—', although we know personally no such reader. If we take so much interest in our town as to be Moderates – or the reverse – we may dislike our opponents. If we be working men we despise the pro-fessional classes and distrust all others. But the individual factor has gone and the power of the individual over the mass.

What prophet shall make London listen to him? Where is London's 'distinguished fellow citizen?' These things are here unknown, and humanity, as the individual, suffers. Economi-cally the city gains. Social reformers, those prophets who see humanity as the gray matter of a theory, would make our corporations more vast, our nations still more boundless, for the sake of fiscal efficiency, for the avoidance of overlapping, in order to make our electric light more cheap or our tram services more adequate. The London County Council should control all South England from the North Foreland to the Land's End. But what we gain thus in the rates we must inevitably lose in our human consciousness and in our civic interests. Londoners, says the Individualist, take no interest in their municipal affairs because the spirit of place has gone. A certain vestry inscribes its dustcarts 'R. B. K.'* – the Royal Borough – but the proud title was gained not by any wish of the inhabitants of the Court suburb, but because of some energetic mayor or borough alderman struggling to gain for himself an infinitesimal moment of Royal attention. What Socrates of London would commence a discourse, 'Oh, men of London!' – 'ὅτι ὑμεις, ὢ ἀνδρες Αθηναῖοι . . .'*

What Londoner, asks the Individualist, cares about Westminster? Nelson did at sea, and some people in Minneapolis,* Minnesota, U.S.A., are thinking about this cradle of the spirit of their race, this old heart of England. But, for the Londoner, there is a convenient station on the Underground, and the name occurs frequently in the endless patter of many bus conductors. So Westminster, as an architectural whole, as a place with strong features, a great history, a place of countless anecdotes whispering from every stone, Westminster is wasted on London. Yet it is the heart of England; the cradle of its laws, of its empire, of its, on the whole, beneficent influence upon the comity of nations. So London extinguishes thoughts about places.

There is in each man of us an Individualist strain more or less strong, and in each, a more or less strong flavour of the Theorist who sees mankind only in the bulk. I imagine the Individualist-half of a man musing like this: 'I inhabit a large, pompous, gloomy London house whose atrocious architecture, in any other spot on the globe, would preclude any idea of my ever countenancing it to the extent of becoming its tenant. Two doors off there lives the greatest violinist in the world, next door an old lady who sat on the knee of George IV; her mind is alive with the most vivid of anecdotes of a century or so – and next door on the other side is a girl with a face as beautiful as that of Helen of Troy,* a delicate and tremulous walk, a proud neck, a radiant costume. Yet, here, I care nothing about any one of them. They are 'the people next door.' For here in London we have no more any neighbours.

'In a smaller community I should choose my house carefully; I should talk to and admire the violinist, listen to and rave about the old lady, and no doubt fall in love with the girl like Helen of Troy. But here, her face will launch no ships; the old lady will find no Boswell* to record her table talk; the violinist will die and, after his name has filled a decently small space in the obituary columns, will go to his rest in some cemetery – and will ensue oblivion. Had he been born in Argos, in a golden age, he would be now the twin of Apollo* – or his name would have been one of the attributes of that composite mystery. So London has dulled my love of the arts, my taste for human gossip – my very manhood.'

'Vous rappelez-vous, dit-il, une réflexion d'Auguste Comte:* (L'humanité est composée de morts et de vivants. Les morts sont de beaucoup le plus nombreux)? Certes, les morts sont de beaucoup les plus nombreux. Par leur multitude et la grandeur du travail accompli, ils sont les plus puissants. Ce sont eux qui gouvernent; nous leur obéissons. Nos maîtres sont sous ces pierres. Voici le législateur qui a fait la loi que je subis aujourd'hui, l'architecte qui a bâti ma maison, le poète qui a créé les illusions qui nous troublent encore, l'orateur qui nous a persuadés avant notre naissance . . . Qu'est-ce qu'une génération de vivants, en comparaison des générations innombrables des morts? Qu'est-ce que notre volonté d'un jour, devant leur volonté mille fois séculaire? . . . Nous révolter contre eux, le pouvons-nous? Nous n'avons pas seulement le temps de leur désobéir!'

'Enfin, vous y venez, docteur Socrate! s'écria Constantin Marc; vous renoncez au progrès, à la justice nouvelle, à la paix du monde, à la libre pensée, vous vous soumettez à la tradition . . .'[1]

This, of course, was written of Paris where, indeed, those at rest are more remembered, since there Parisians hold once each year a tremendous festival of the dead. But it might stand at least as well, in those Westminster cloisters, for the shadows that are for ever flying over this London of ours. It epitomises

---

[1] 'Do you remember, he said, a reflexion of Auguste Comte: (Humanity is composed of the dead and of the living. The dead are much the more numerous)? Certainly the dead are much the more numerous. By their multitude, and on account of the greatness of the work they have accomplished, they are the more powerful. It is they who govern: we obey them. Our masters are beneath these stones. Here lie the legislator who made the law I submit to today, the architect who built my house, the poet who created the illusions that trouble us still, the orator who influenced our minds before we were born . . . What is one generation of the living compared to the innumerable generations of the dead? What is our will, dating only from today, before their wills that are a thousand centuries old? Revolt against them? Are we strong enough? We have not even time to disobey them.' 'There you are then, Doctor Socrates,' cried Constantin Marc; 'you renounce Progress, the New Justice, the World's Peace, Free Thought; you submit yourself to Tradition.'

the two habits of mind. For the Individualist, the humanist, sees his dead and his living as human beings: Law givers, architects, poets who trouble us still with their Illusions, orators who provide the catch-words that still influence us and our minds. He may stand, that Individualist, for the London that is eternally passing and past. He sees figures in that mist. But the words of his opponent, the man of the future; 'Progress', the 'New Spirit of Justice', the 'World's Peace', are always abstractions. Looking forward, looking into the mists of the future, the future whose men are unborn, he sees no figures. And looking at Westminster Abbey he thinks of Building Enactments.

And there, where the great towers rise up, grim and black, where the memorials cower at the base of walls grim and black, where fountains stand in the weeping light of obscure and useless cloisters that suggest the gaunt and blackened skeletons of obsolete faiths, obsolete pursuits, obsolete hopes and obsolete despairs; where there are all sorts of courts and alleys of old houses that seem to whisper of faded virtues, faded vices, faded pleasures, dead crimes – that seem to whisper of all the Past, and that are being swept away along with all their 'character', all their romance, by Building Improvement Schemes – in that Westminster, where suddenly you come upon boys' figures, flickering in white jerseys, playing football in a small square, the very heart of England, there the old Individualist and the man whose eyes look forward may very well confute each other unanswerably. For, says the Theorist that is in all of us, in that abbey and in that cloister, how many legislators will not be found, venial, selfish, treacherous, legislators who inflicted upon us laws under which we still groan? how many poets who wrote ignoble verse from which the art of poetry still suffers? how many orators who started ignoble, base, and harmful catch-words that still sway our mobs, that still govern our corporate lives?

And, looking at those school boys playing football, your Individualist will retort: 'Observe that red-headed boy with a squint, with the low forehead, the bad skull; observe that good, honest, stupid looking muscular boy by the goal posts; observe that dark, shifty, clever little rat of a chap dodging like a weasel with the ball: what will your Corporations of the future be like when those are the units, when you have swept away the love of place with your improvement schemes, when you have swept away all fear of public opinion by weakening our every individual tie? Do you imagine, really, that "Tomorrow will be like today but much more sweet?" Do you imagine that poor humanity will ever be other than poor humanity?'

So the shadow passes over their argument – the shadow of the Passing that seems, in that heart of the nation, to be for ever on the point of overwhelming those old things. Yet, as a matter of fact, it never really overwhelms them until the new things have already grown old. For all of old Westminster will not be swept away, there will still remain a fragment of the ancient monastery wall, pieces of the cloisters, old Georgian courts, when already the improved buildings of today will be found to be inadequate, insanitary, smoke-begrimed for certain, pictur- esque probably, possibly glamorous, and surely very old. For once a building rests upon the soil of London, it seems to grapple to the earth as if with hooks far stronger than steel; just as once a man is at rest upon his bier he is so strong that it needs four others to take him to his resting place. And, upon the whole, the Philosopher in us, the part which observes passion- lessly, will be upon the side of the friend of the future.

Poor humanity, which works out its own destinies, has given its vote unconsciously against the Individualist. Catch-words, the illusions of the poets, the streets paved with gold, have drawn these great bodies into this great city. And, inasmuch as the Philosopher is a person who accepts the accomplished things, he must accept along with it the Corporations, the gradual death of altruisms, of creeds, of humanities and of the individual as a factor of public life. The great figures of the last century – like the Ruskins, the Bismarcks, the Napoleons, the Tennysons, the Gladstones* – have passed away, because no man can now appeal largely enough to affect the immense public. What single great figure is there in the world of whom it could be said that the noise of his death being cried in a suburban street of liver- coloured brick boxes would cause half a dozen blinds to be pulled down, or half a dozen figures to come to the doors to hear the news? There is no such name.[1]

---

[1] This of course is an exaggeration on the part of the Philosopher, who looking too closely at the present forgets that one of his young friends – or he himself – may stand revealed to Posterity as a great figure. But, except, perhaps, for a single politician, it is difficult to find one man whose name today would be familiar in every street of this London.

So it seems as if the Great Figure as a human factor has gone, and it seems as if London will never again know another Dr Johnson, although at a hundred street corners you might meet men as wise, as mordant, as dogmatic, as unhappy, as vivacious, as great Figures.

This, however, is not an indictment of London. It is rather the mere statement of losses in a great balance sheet. We have lost great figures, old buildings, all touch with history, much of Christian kindness, much of our fear of public opinion, much of our capacity for interest in our fellow men, much of our powers of abstract reasoning, much of our old faiths.

We have gained a certain amount of public efficiency, the avoidance of much 'overlapping', a dim sort of idea of how the world may be carried forward, a comfortable indifference to many sham observances, class distinctions, and personal infringements of the social codes; and gradually we are evolving a practical means of living together in the great city. If the profit side of the account sheet seems unsubstantial, that is only because of poor humanity's innate inability to see, to under- stand, the good of its own day – because of the sentimentality of poor humanity that will continue to think an old faith more attractive than an efficient system of local government. We are, after all, still troubled by the illusions of our dead poets. So speaks the Philosopher, who stands midway between the Indi- vidualist and the Theorist . . .

Outside in the woods it is spring, and Nature is preparing for her tremendous waste of individual leaves, birds, gnats, and small and great beasts. There may be sun there, and certainly the sap is stirring, or there may be cloud shapes to be seen, and there is always a sky. But I stand in my window and look down the long perspective of a street. It vanishes, dwindles, grows uncertain, and fades into a black and uniform opacity. There is no sky, or the sky has descended upon earth like a gray pall. There is no colour visible anywhere but gray save for the red of a letter box that seems to float, blotted, in vapour, and the white triangular tops of the lamp-posts. Through the gloom hail falls steadily and close, like fine rain, and behind it everything is flat, dim, as if the house fronts, the garden walls, the pavements, were cloudy forms printed in gray upon a large cloth.

Suddenly spaces exists: it is as if a red torch were shaken in the air and quenched. That is lightning, a reminder of the outside world that we have half forgotten. A broad shaft of sunlight reddens for an instant, in the distance, the white square face of a house whose dark windows seem to peer back like gloomy eyes: it fades, and the eye is drawn upwards to an immense and sullen glow, the edge of a heavy cloud that towers perpendicularly on high. The vast pall of vapour that over-spreads London, becomes for that moment visible and manifest on account of that rift in its surface. It joins again, the blackness descends once more, the hail, the colourlessness of all the world. The houses once more look like clouds.

And indeed it is impossible, without an effort, to dissociate in our minds the idea of London from the idea of a vast cloud beneath a cloud as vast. The memory cannot otherwise conceive of all these gray buildings, of all these gray people. You do not, for instance, call up in your mind all the houses you would pass between Charing Cross and Knightsbridge: they fade into one mass, and because that mass is one you will never touch and finger, it seems cloudlike enough. But all the limitless stretches of roofs that you have never seen, the streets that you will never travel, the miles and miles of buildings, the myriads of plane-trees, of almonds, of elms – all these appalling regions of London that to every individual of us must remain unknown and untraversed – all those things fuse in our minds into one cloud. And the Corporations, the Water Boards, the Dock Boards, the Railway Organisations, the bodies of men who keep the parks in order, the armies who sweep in the streets – all these are cloudlike too. They seem unnatural, all these things, and London itself is at times apt to seem unreal. So that when we come across a park with sharp folds in the land, sharp dips, sudden rises, it is almost astonishing that anything so natural and so real should remain in the heart of this cloud beneath a cloud. For, little by little, the Londoner comes to forget that his London is built upon real earth: he forgets that under the pavements there are hills, forgotten water courses, springs and marshland.

And beneath and amongst all those clouds – thunderclouds, the cloud of buildings, the clouds of corporations – there hurries still the great swarm of tiny men and women, each one hugging desperately his own soul, his own hopes, his own passions, his own individuality. To destroy these individualities is impossible.

I am acquainted with a reformer, however, whose ideal of impersonality is so close, so stern, and so unflinching that he would abolish all names of persons, substituting numbers. He would have all men and women who perform any public functions, all candidates for State examinations, go masked and dressed in cloaks that should destroy all distinction of figure and limbs. Physical beauty must be concealed, physical defects must be 'levelled up'; personality must go.

This, of course, is *la justice nouvelle* – the new justice; and it is obvious that these impersonal corporations of the future cannot work ideally without some such precautions against favouritism, or against the 'personal magnetism' that gives sway over crowds. But, in the meantime, those days seem far enough off. Our street-corner Johnsons if they cannot any longer get the ear of the world are none the less Johnsons; our unpublished poets are none the less poets. It is only the audience that is unreachable, and perhaps it is only the world that is the loser. But, after all, no doubt it matters little. What is of importance is whether the sum of human happiness be affected in this great town.

Westminster Building Improvements sweep away whole crowds of human associations: they run up barracks that apparently are distinguished by no single merit. But those Georgian houses that are disappearing, swept away in their day houses older, streets narrower, halls where still greater history was made. Those Georgian streets, courts, culs-de-sac stood mostly for brocaded coats, for powdered wigs, for brilliant talkers, great gamblers, women very dissolute and men very coarse; they stood, in fact, rather for still-life gossip than for national actions, rather for Memoirs than for 'History'. But the older streets that they displaced stood for kings, great nobles, great churchmen. Westminster Hall* – which has given place to that great ugly box with its futile tracery of misplaced ornaments – Westminster Hall saw History. The times then were less spacious, and, London being so much smaller, the really insignificant acts of kings, nobles, and churchmen 'counted' to an extent that no single act of any one man could today count.

And that tendency is inevitable as the world grows broader, as the cities stretch out. 'History' becomes impossible. It was already, as far as London was concerned, over and done with when the young Pretender*failed in the 45. Had he taken

London, sacked the City, crowned himself in Westminster, misruled, caused new revolutions to foment, new deeds of blood and rapine to set the stones of the Court whispering, history might have continued to be made until near our own day. Nay, even London itself might have been checked for a century or two of its growth, since turbulence and the civil wars inevitable to the Stuarts would have delayed the coming of Arkwrights and Kays,* have put back the clock of our industrial develop-ments, have influenced the fate of the whole world. But history of that type ended with Culloden.

The Chronicler had to turn his pen to the accounts of the great impersonal movements, as: 'It was then that cotton spinning was established'; 'It was then that, great depression having overtaken the agricultural districts, immense bodies of the rural populations moved into the great towns.' The race of memoir writers began to discover the witty, the sensible, the profusely dressed, or the profligate Great Figures. Now those, too, are done with, since, as the background grows, the figure dwindles in proportion and loses its importance amongst the vaster crowds upon the canvas. We have no longer, as it were, pictures of Sir Thomas Gresham,* M, burning in the presence of the King the King's I.O.U.s to a fabulous amount. Instead, in the historic picture of today, it is 'the Sovereign' (who is now much less a human being than the representative of a political theory) 'attending service at St Paul's, met by the Lord Mayor' (whose name nine-tenths of London ignores), 'the Sheriffs and the Corporation of the City of London'. The City itself has no longer any visible bounds, walls, or demarcations; it is a postal district, 'E.C.', an abstraction still playing at being an individ-uality. On our new chronicle-canvas the Lord Mayor is a tiny speck that Sir Thomas Gresham, M, of the older picture could swallow; the Sovereign is not much larger; the spectators make a large bulk, and the major part of the composition is filled up with London, the impersonal buildings, the columns, pilasters, the shop fronts, the advertisement posters – the cloud.

The man with an eye to the future may even wonder whether those heavy buildings – that cloud pressing so heavily upon the hills and the marshes of the ancient river mouth – may not be little more than an obsolete incubus, or at least an obsolescent one. The point is whether the 'old building', the heavy perma-nent mass of stone, timber, and brick is not a mere survival of the worship of the spirit of the hearth. The point is whether, except for that sentimental reason, portable buildings of corrugated iron, of woven wire – even for the summer, of paper – might not be more sanitary, more in keeping with the spirit of the age, less of a tie to the people of the future, our children; for as London weakens the human ties, so it weakens the spirit of the family and the spirit of hospitality. I knew, for instance, an old gentleman who would never quarrel with anyone in his own house, because of his respect for his own roof; he would quarrel with no one under a friend's roof out of respect for his friend's. He would not even write an unfriendly letter in his own or a friend's house. Consequently if he wanted to 'have it out with' a man he had to invite him to some public place, or, if he wanted to write to the *Times*, denouncing some public 'job', he would retire to the nearest hotel and call for a pint of claret, pens and paper. He would himself acknowledge that these proceedings were rather exaggerated, but his instinctive feelings in the matter were so strong that not even the necessity of a bath chair in extreme old age could prevent his going to that hotel for that purpose.

That feeling, I fancy, has died out, or is dying, in London. We have slackened all these ties, and the sanguine reformer foresees also a gradual decay of respect for family portraits. It is, after all, to house heirlooms, he says, that we build great houses or inhabit them. We collect our grandfather's old, too heavy, insect-infected chairs and chiffoniers, punch bowls, spoons or bedsteads. These things are full of cobwebs, dirt, microbes; and the old houses, that are largely our ideals still, are still more insanitary and demoralising. We have even a London proverb: 'Three moves are worse than a fire'; that is because we have too much of this unwieldy bric-a-brac. Really, says this reformer, we ought in the interests of hygiene to cultivate an extreme cleanliness, and that is only possible with a minimum of furniture. We should promote, as far as possible, portability in our houses, because ground that has been dwelt upon too long loses its resilience, its power of assimilating human debris.

Thus we must pull down our London; burn our ancestral furniture; melt down our punch bowls; recognise that our associations as far as they are ancestral, are so many cobwebs; and send the best of old family portraits into the Museums. – These last will soon – says the Reformer, seeing his dream as a

reality of to-morrow – be the sole heavy buildings to raise lofty
roofs and turrets above the plateau of small houses – houses of
aluminium, of woven wire, of corrugated iron, of paper pulp;
small houses containing only a mat or two, a vase for flowers, a
cooking stove; houses that we shall pack on to motor cars when
the fit moves us to go out into the fields for a month or two, or
when business becomes slack in London itself, or when we
desire to 'air' our camping site.

The obsolete system of land tenure would facilitate this; the
growing restlessness of the people; the desire for change of
scene; the dearth of domestic labour; and, above all, according
to this Reformer, the fact that no house *ought* to be more than
twenty years old.

I suppose that such a London with its portable houses, its
masked and numbered inhabitants (perhaps we should arrive at
such a pitch of impersonality that a child would recognise its
mother, like a sheep, by the sense of smell) – this London would
be sane, sanitary, and beneficent to the human race. Most of us,
being poor humanity, a prey to the illusions of dead poets, will
shudder at what is raw and naked in this idea. But what is the
alternative London that is offered us by the man who upholds
the Past?

It is a vast stretch of mounds, a gigantic quagmire with here
and there a pillar of a mediaeval church serving as a perch for a
hawk's nest, and here and there a clump of trees, descendants of
those in our parks, in whose shadow foxes and badgers shall
herd, on whose tops the herons shall nest. The praiser of Times
Past will tell us that the breed is deteriorating physically: it is
growing hopelessly neurasthenic; it is losing its business energy.
It has sapped all the blood from the counties; it is closing its
doors to emigrants from the countries. It is breaking with the
old Social Conventions: it is running blindly to perdition.

And indeed this picture of an immense Town, shut off from
the rest of the world, black, walled in, peopled by gibbering
neurasthenics, a prey to hysterias, useless for work, getting no
pleasures from horrible self indulgences – this image of a City
of dreadful Night* is appalling enough. And its logical end
would be that wide desolation, those mounds, those quagmires.

For, supposing that Physical Deterioration to exist, we must
lose our business capacities; a sound mind going with a healthy
body, London must lose her trade. The small houses on the

outskirts would first lose their populations. Imagine then all those horrible little hutches that have spread out over Essex. – Slates will come loose, rain trickle in, frosts split asunder the walls, naked rafters clutch at the skies, until at last all that great uninhabited region of damp ground will have its thin plastering of rubble, of rubbish, levelled on the ground and making small mounds for the couch grass to cover with its thick tangle. And, as trade ebbs and ebbs from this city of neurasthenics, the Vestries, the Corporations, the Conservancies,* will lack the money with which to fight the Thames, that great friend that made London, that great enemy that ultimately shall overwhelm it. A very little want of attention to the sewers, the embankments and the up-river locks would swamp at each tide all the City and all London. The sliding sands would get into motion beneath St Paul's; all the hidden streams and rivulets that London has forgotten would swell, burst their bonds, and beneath the ground eat into the foundations of the houses. (I know, for instance, a London dwelling where a spring has suddenly and invincibly burst its way through the kitchen stairs so that the house has had to be abandoned.)

We who walk about the streets forget the elements; we hardly ever realise by what minute and meticulous patching up the great city is rendered water-tight and air-tight – with tiny slates on the roofs and tiny tiles in the sewers, or with what constant filling up of fresh materials the roadway of the Victoria Embankment is kept from becoming a mere swamp. But you may realise this last if you go, in heavy weather upon any kind of vehicle, along this the worst of London's great roads that flaunts itself against the remorseless forces of nature.

And who, says the praiser of Times Past, would live in London if it did not pay him? London has become a mere bazaar, a mere market. Its associations have gone; its humanity has gone; it is uninhabitable for its atmosphere, for its inhuman solitude, for its indifference to architecture, for its pulling down of old courts.

So, in this image, London, an immense galleon, drifts down the tideway of the ages, threatened imminently by those black and sulphurous clouds, Neurasthenia, Decay, and the waters of the Earth. So, in the other image, it will – humanity being redeemable – become a gigantic, bright, sanitary and sane congeries of little white houses that can be folded up and carried off in the night. On the one hand there will at last be Rest in London; on the other – humanity being redeemable – there will never be rest at all, but the great city will go staggering along through a series of changes in the nature of man.

But the contemplative portion of our psychologies seems to reply to these extremists that there is never any change in the nature of man. Furniture is, it is true, getting lighter and more flimsy, but the natural man will go on accumulating as much of it as he can, or as much as his servants or his wife can dust. And his grandson will go on – with variations dictated by the Fashions of his day – treasuring such of his grandfather's heavier and most costly pieces as he imagines will do credit to the family. There passes one's window every morning a Charity School: a hundred and twenty girls, each in gray skirts, gray cloaks, heavy boots, and straw hats. They have been drilled to adopt as nearly as possible a stereotyped walk, an odd sort of swing from the hips, and shuffle of the toes on the ground. They have eaten the same food, slept in the same long dormitories. – Turning off one's street there is a long narrow road of small houses, each precisely alike in dingy and indistinguishable architecture, each the same in rent, in chimneys, in window space. – Here, then, are stereotyped citizens and stereotyped houses.

Yet, in spite of the efforts of the good nuns to sap the individual spark in each of those girls, each has a different swing of the hips, cock of the shoulder, glance from the eye. And, in spite of the effort of the architect or jobbing builder to render each of those house-boxes indistinguishable from the other, each has an entirely different atmosphere. Here a door has been painted green, here a handle has been polished till it shines like gold, here the curtains are clean, here a window has been broken and replaced with gummed paper. So that from each of those houses a soul seems to peep forth, differing from each other soul. My bedroom window being very high, I look down into innumerable tiny garden plots when I dress. In the first the tenant is out every morning directing his gardener to put in bulbs, to roll a tiny shell-path, to re-arrange a rockery, to stick up little boxes for the starlings to nest in. In the next the tenant has had the whole space tiled and reddened to save the trouble of attending to it. In the next there is nothing but blackened and sodden grass. Thus, in these stereotyped pocket-handkerchief squares of a quarter where one would imagine the solid Middle Class to be most uniform and alike, individualities stamp themselves upon the very waste ground.

So that, to those who love their fellow-men, it seems unnecessary to fear much. Even in the Utopia London of masks, dominoes, and, in place of names, numbers, it seems unlikely that one pair of eyes will not gleam more brightly through the eyelets, one domino be worn more jauntily, or one voice be the more thrilling. And the range being less wide, the minute differences will be all the more apparent. Even today class and class of us go seeking appointments in uniforms that, if individuality could be blotted out, would surely do it. We go to offices in high hats, frock coats, trousers cut alike, or in bowlers, broadcloth, or corduroys. But there is difference enough between wearer and wearer of these uniforms.

Tall blocks of office buildings are crushing out the associations of the Westminster courts, alleys, and squares. We see terracotta ornamental excrescences, meaning nothing to us; heavy masses that, to those of us who care about architectural proportions, are repulsive, because, for us, they have no associations. The Memoirists have not yet written them up. But to our great grandchildren these excrescences will have meanings and associations, these heavinesses will be suggestive, because we, their ancestors, lived amongst these things our pathetic, petty, and futile lives.

When Westminster was still an ecclesiastical islet* with a drawbridge, odd roads and quaint figures, there were men who grumbled because apple orchards had taken the place of swamps where the wild geese cried all night. And there were monks who rejoiced that new stone salting houses had taken the place of the old, rotting wooden curing huts. They thought their houses looked better, just as nearly all London thinks the office buildings look better than the eighteenth-century rabbit-warrens of small houses. And there were others who foresaw gigantic and impersonal futures for the Church, the Minster, or for Mankind. And your Abbot Samson* found his Jocelynd of Brakelond to be a Boswell for him.

Even the Great Figure still lives: for humanity craves for admiration to give and to take. In the streets you will still hear: 'Oh, such a one: he's a *one-er*', in the Clubs they still say: 'So and so is rather a good man, isn't he?' whether So and So be a surgeon, an admiral, or the administrator of a province in Upper Burma. So the populations of the many towns that form London jog along together towards their inevitable rest. The associations that are forming around our Street Improvements are none the less poignant, because they are less historic in the large. For the poignancy of these things comes from the man, without regard to the object to which it attaches.

These sayings without doubt are so many platitudes: but if we consider Rest in London, we have to consider the Future, and to consider the Future, we must deal in generalisations, which are brave platitudes. There remains then the question of Physical Deterioration. 'That Neurasthenia joke,' said a modern doctor, a man looking half Jew, half negroid, but young and alert with beady eyes behind large spectacles, 'It's as old as the hills. Jezebel* was Neurasthenic; so was Lot's wife* when she looked back; so was the writer of the book of Job.* So was Edward II;* so was Shakespeare, or whoever wrote *Timon of Athens*.* If we've deteriorated physically, when did the deterioration begin?' He paced up and down his consulting-room smiling, and tapped his patient on the shoulder with a stethoscope. 'We've improved: we're improving. Why, my dear sir, what was old age in the mediaeval centuries? A man – a king – was worn out, crippled with rheumatism, too heavy-bellied to mount his horse before he was forty-five. As to the common people, they died like flies: they had no stamina, no power of resisting disease. Town life isn't unhealthy: the art of sanitation did not begin until the towns grew large. Did you ever see an old farm-house? Where did they build them? Always in hollows, in muddy, airless bottoms, to be near water – you understand: near water – and they drained into that water – and they were plague houses all of them.

'Did you ever have to do with a sick farm labourer? Those fellows! Why, they fold their hands and die for a touch of liver. Their life doesn't hold them because it contains no interest. Half their healthy hours are spent in mooning and brooding: they all suffer from dyspepsia because of their abominable diet of cheese and tea. Why, I'd rather attend fifty London street rats with half a lung apiece than one great hulking farm bailiff. Those are the fellows, after all, the London scaramouches,* for getting over an illness.

'Don't you see, my dear sir, your problem is to breed disease-resisting men, and you won't do it from men who mope about fields and hedges. No! modern life is a question of towns. Purify them if you can: get rid of smoke and foul air if you can. But breed a race fitted to inhabit them in any case.'

That indeed is the problem which is set before London – the apotheosis of modern life. For there is no ignoring the fact that mankind elects to live in crowds. If London can evolve a town type London will be justified of its existence. In these great movements of mortality the preacher and the moralist are powerless. If a fitted race can be bred, a race will survive, multiply and carry on vast cities. If no such race arrive the city must die. For, sooner or late, the drain upon the counties must cease: there will be no fresh blood to infuse. If it be possible, in these great rule of thumb congeries, 'sanitary conditions' must be enforced; rookeries must be cleared out; so many cubic feet of air must be ensured for each individual. (And it must be remembered that, for the Christian era, this is a new problem. No occidental cities, great in the modern sense, have existed, none have begun to exist until the beginning of the Commercial Ages. The problem is so very young that we have only just begun to turn our attention to it.)

But, if the rest that comes with extinction is not to be the ultimate lot of London, the problem must solve itself either here or there – in the evolution either of a healthy city or of a race with a strong hold upon life. We know that equatorial swamps have evolved tribes, short legged, web-footed, fitted to live in damp, in filth, in perpetual miasmas. There is no reason therefore why London should not do as much for her children. That would indeed be her justification, the apology for her existence.

The creatures of the future will come only when our London indeed is at rest. And, be they large-headed, short legged, narrow-chested, and, by our standards, hideous and miserable, no doubt they will find among themselves women to wive with, men to love and dispute for, joys, sorrows, associations, Great Figures, histories – a London of their own, graves of their own, and rest. Our standards will no longer prevail, our loves will be dead; it will scarcely matter much to us whether Westminster Abbey stand or be pulled down: it will scarcely matter to us whether the portraits of our loves be jeered at as we jeer at the portraits of the loves, wives, mistresses and concubines of Henry VIII.* Some of us seek to govern the Future: may their work prosper in their hands; some of us seek to revive, to bathe in, the spirit of the Past: surely great London will still, during their lives, hold old courts, old stones, old stories, old memories. Some of us seek relief from our cares in looking upon the present of our times. We may be sure that to these unambitious, to these humble, to these natural men, who sustain their own lives through the joys, the sorrows, and the personalities of the mortal creatures that pass them in the street, wait upon them at table, deliver their morning bread, stand next to them in public-house bars – to these London with its vastness that will last their day, will grant the solace of unceasing mortals to be interested in.

In the end we must all leave London; for all of us it must be again London from a distance, whether it be a distance of six feet underground, or whether we go to rest somewhere on the other side of the hills that ring in this great river basin. For us, at least, London, its problems, its past, its future, will be at rest. At nights the great blaze will shine up at the clouds; on the sky there will still be that brooding and enigmatic glow, as if London with a great ambition strove to grasp at Heaven with arms that are shafts of light. That is London writing its name upon the clouds.

And in the hearts of its children it will still be something like a cloud – a cloud of little experiences, of little personal impressions,* of small, futile things that, seen in moments of stress and anguish, have significances so tremendous and meanings so poignant. A cloud – as it were of the dust of men's lives.

NOTES

***

p. iii   A Traveller ... to be sad: Shakespeare, *As You Like It*, IV.i.22

p. xxx   Dedication to Mrs William Martindale: Ford's mother-in-law, widow of Dr William Martindale (d. 1902), an eminent chemist and associate of Lister. The Martindales had lived in New Cavendish Street, Marylebone Road, and at Winchelsea.

p. 4   Dr Johnson's chair: Samuel Johnson (1709–84), lexicographer and man of letters, presided over his literary club at the Turk's Head in Gerrard Street, Soho, 1764–83. In *The Critical Attitude* Ford called him 'the greatest, because the most representative, of all English figures'.

p. 5   the Tower: fortress built by William the Conqueror around 1078 to overawe the inhabitants of London.

p. 8   Sweeny Todd ... Barber: subject of the macabre street ballad of the Demon Barber of Fleet Street, who with the help of Mrs Lovett made his victims into meat pies.

p. 8   spring-pistols: toy guns.

p. 8   alley-taws: glass marbles (as referred to in Dickens, *Pickwick Papers*, Ch. 34).

p. 9   the Monument: the column, probably designed by Sir Christopher Wren, erected in 1671–7 north of London Bridge near the house in Pudding Lane where the Great Fire of London broke out in 1666.

p. 9   his own Stour ... or Adur: rivers in, respectively, Essex, Yorkshire (unless the East Anglian Ouse is meant), and Sussex.

p. 10   Gower's tombs and Botticelli's: the tomb of the poet John Gower (?1325–1408) in what is now Southwark Cathedral, and the paintings by Sandro Botticelli (1444–1510), the great Italian Renaissance artist, in the National Gallery in Trafalgar Square.

p. 10   waxen effigies: in Madame Tussaud's Waxworks, founded by

Marie Tussaud (1760–1850) in Baker Street in 1833 and transferred to Marylebone Road in 1884.

p. 10 *alt-bier* **soup:** made from heavy top-fermented German beer.

p. 10 **Millbank National Gallery:** the Tate Gallery on Millbank, built as a gift of Sir Henry Tate in 1897 to house the national collection of British art.

p. 10 **'Underground':** the first section of the London underground railway, the Metropolitan, from Paddington to Farringdon Street, was opened in 1863; the Inner Circle was complete by 1884; and the first electric railway, the City and South London line, from King William Street to Stockwell, began operating in 1890.

p. 11 **Crosses:** particularly, perhaps, Charing Cross, the last of the Queen Eleanor Crosses marking the stages of the Queen's funeral procession from Lincoln to Westminster, originally in what is now Trafalgar Square, but re-erected in substitute form outside Charing Cross Station in Victorian times.

p. 11 *arrière boutique:* back shop.

p. 12 **Mormon and Mussulman:** the American Mormon Church of Jesus Christ of Latter-Day Saints was founded by Joseph Smith in 1830, and subsequently transferred to Salt Lake City, Utah, by Brigham Young. Mussulman is a Persian term for Mohammedan.

p. 12 **Agapemonite:** member of a fanatical revivalist sect, started in 1849 and reconstituted at Clapton in 1890, where it enjoyed considerable notoriety before disappearing without trace.

p. 13 **Junker:** Prussian aristocrat.

p. 14 **Nijni Novgorod:** now the Russian city of Gorki.

p. 14 **a great Gothic cathedral:** Old St Paul's, destroyed in the Great Fire of 1666, and replaced by Sir Christopher Wren's Classical building (1675–1711).

p. 14 **the diarists:** John Evelyn (1620–1706), and more importantly Samuel Pepys (1633–1703), Clerk of the King's Ships (1660) and Secretary of the Admiralty (1686), whose diary records the Plague, the Great Fire, and the Restoration of Charles II.

p. 14 **Defoe:** Daniel Defoe (?1661–1731), journalist and novelist, whose fictions often assume the guise of genuine memoirs of the period.

p. 14 Hogarth ... Albert Smith: William Hogarth (1697–1764), painter and caricaturist, celebrated for *The Rake's Progress* and other satirical pictures of London life. In 1749, during a visit to France, he was arrested as a spy for sketching the English arms on the old gate of Calais, and put on a ship back to England. His later picture *Gate of Calais* pillories the local inhabitants. Albert Smith (1816–60), author and entertainer, was known for his dramatic depictions of English life at the Egyptian Hall in Piccadilly, 1851–8.

p. 14 Dickens: Charles Dickens's *Uncommercial Traveller*, a series of sketches of London life and character from his weekly paper *All the Year Round*, first appeared in volume form in 1861. In Ch. 7 he travels to France, setting out over Shooter's Hill in south-east London on the Dover Road. Is Ford's reference to Denmark Hill a slip?

p. 15 Lutetia: the ancient name for Paris, first recorded by Caesar: also the name of a Symbolist review, 1883–6.

p. 15 figure on the reverse ... coins: Britannia, on the old penny piece.

p. 15 Mercator's projection: Gerardus Mercator, otherwise Gerhard Kremer (1512–94), the Flemish geographer, whose 'projections' or maps established cartography on a firm mathematical and astronomical basis.

p. 15 hay-cocks: conical heaps of hay.

p. 16 Boulevard Haussman ... Pyramids: to the north of the Opéra, one of the great Boulevards opened up in Paris by Baron Haussman (1809–91), Napoleon III's Prefect of the Seine Department, during the Second Empire. The Rue des Pyramides runs north from the Rue de Rivoli towards the Opéra.

p. 17 pabula: foodstuffs.

p. 17 Garden Cities: this movement, a reaction against the notorious slums of Victorian London, had led to the creation of Bedford Park, Chiswick (1875), by Norman Shaw, and at the time Ford was writing the Hampstead Garden Suburb was under construction. The first two factory estates planned as garden suburbs were at Port Sunlight (1888) and Bourneville (1895).

p. 17 Armageddon: the final conflict between the nations, foretold in *Revelation*, xvi:16.

p. 18   hopping season: the Kentish hop-picking season provided opportunities for London working-class holidays until quite recently.

p. 18   tabernacle in the synagogue: the successful Jew, Ford is saying, will always hark back to the customs, language and ceremonies of his Jewish upbringing.

p. 19   Bill Sikes and Fagin's academy: see Dickens, *Oliver Twist*, Ch. 9.

p. 19   Cimmerian: plunged in darkness, as of the ancient tribe of the Cimmerii, supposed to live in perpetual darkness.

p. 19   Cruikshank: George Cruikshank (1792–1878), engraver and book illustrator, particularly of Dickens's early novels.

p. 20   Poor Law Relief: since the Act of 1834, satirised in *Oliver Twist*, poor law relief had been progressively ameliorated during the Victorian period. In the year Ford was writing (1905), a new Commission was set up by Balfour's government to study the working of the Poor Laws and methods for meeting distress caused by industrial depression and unemployment.

p. 20   Sodom and Gomorrah: the cities of abomination, destroyed by God in *Genesis*, Ch. 19.

p. 21   Mansion House: built 1739–53 as the official residence of the Lord Mayor of London.

p. 21   Spring Gardens: a street off Whitehall, near the Admiralty Arch, where the original offices of the London County Council were situated before they were moved to the new County Hall on the South Bank after the First World War.

p. 23   It has no Acropolis . . . Valhalla: the citadel of Ancient Athens. Ford's point is that unlike Athens, Rome, Paris, or even St Petersburg, London has no central focal point. Neither Westminster Abbey, the resting place of its illustrious dead, nor the Houses of Parliament, were built with that intention. Valhalla in Norse mythology was the palace in which the souls of the slain were feasted.

p. 25   'shays': a shadow or faint ray of light (Kentish or Surrey dialect). Ford's use of dialect words and colloquialisms adds much to the tonal variety and vitality of his impressionism.

p. 25   Administrative County: the London County Council had been set up in 1888.

p. 25 **Essex flats:** flatlands on the north side of the Thames estuary.

p. 26 **zenanas:** Hindu word for the women's quarters in an Indian house.

p. 27 **Nine Elms, Barn Elms:** the former, in Battersea, became a railway marshalling yard, the latter, in Richmond, a water-works.

p. 28 **The electric tram:** first introduced in Birkenhead by the American engineer George Francis Train, tramways had spread all over London by the turn of the century.

p. 28 **Welsh Harp:** public house in Hendon, near the site of the present Welsh Harp Reservoir.

p. 28 **Apsley House:** the London residence of the Duke of Wellington at Hyde Park Corner, originally built by Adam 1771–8, and now a museum.

p. 31 **knifeboard:** double bench running lengthways down the top deck of an omnibus.

p. 31 **the Bank:** the Bank of England in Threadneedle Street, at this period still the building of Sir John Soane (1753–1837).

p. 32 **a pikey:** turnpike traveller or tramp (Kent and Surrey slang).

p. 33 **the trial of Count Königsmarck:** Thomas Thynne, of Longleat in Wiltshire (1648–82), a supporter of the Duke of Monmouth, secretly married the widow of Lord Ogle, Elizabeth, daughter of the 11th Earl of Northumberland and heiress to the Percy estates, but the marriage was not consummated. Thynne's claim to his wife's property was upheld after a legal battle; but he was subsequently assassinated (1682), and one of his wife's unsuccessful suitors, a Swedish nobleman named Carl Johann von Koenigsmark, was implicated in the crime and committed to Newgate. The three assassins were put on trial and condemned to death; but Koenigsmark, though charged as an accessory, was unexpectedly acquitted and left the country. The affair stirred up much popular feeling on account of Thynne's connection with Monmouth, and he was accorded a monument in Westminster Abbey on which is carved a representation of his violent death. Ford seems to have come across one or other of the two folio volumes published about the trial in 1682; but the affair is also recorded in memoirs and diaries of the time.

p. 33 **Casanova:** Giovanni Giocomo Casanova (1725–98), known for his *Memoirs* recording his amorous adventures.

p. 33   Mr Round's 'Commune of London': published 1899 by John Horace Round (1854–1928), the medieval historian, and notable for its study of the early history of London.

p. 33   Angevin kings: the Plantagenets.

p. 33   Congreve ... Richardson: all the writers Ford mentions were given a ready welcome in France: William Congreve (1670–1729), the Restoration dramatist; Philip Dormer Stanhope, 4th Earl of Chesterfield (1694–1773), best known for his 'Letters' relating to the education of his godson; Edward Gibbon (1737–94), author of *The Decline and Fall of the Roman Empire*; and Samuel Richardson (1689–1761), the novelist, author of *Pamela* and *Clarissa*.

p. 34   footnote: Ford's summary of the political and economic significance of the capital from the middle ages to the final extinction of the old order (as he saw it) with the failure of the Stuart cause in 1746 illustrates his growing interest in the development of English character and institutions before, and after, the breach with Rome at the Reformation. After the Revolution of 1688, the principal lenders to government were organised in the Bank of England (1694), and this led to an alliance between the King's ministers and the City, which was predominantly Whig in sympathy and opposed to the Old Pretender. Thereafter, any return of the Stuarts posed a threat to the financial stability of the City, as it was feared that he would repudiate the National Debt.

p. 34   jades of Belgia: Dutch hacks or horses.

p. 35   Taylor the water poet: John Taylor (1580–1653), a Thames waterman, gained the patronage of Ben Jonson and made a name for himself as a poet and organiser of pageants. Later, he lived in Oxford and ran an inn in Long Acre. His collected works were published in 1630.

p. 35   wharfingers: wharf owners.

p. 36   'workmen's fares': first introduced in London in 1864, and consolidated in the Cheap Trains Act of 1883 to encourage workmen to migrate into the suburbs.

p. 36   Somerset House: on the Strand, with a frontage to the Thames, built on the site of the Protector Somerset's residence to the designs of Sir William Chambers from 1776, and intended to house a number of public administrative departments.

p. 36 'ceilings by Adams': Robert Adam (1728–92), Scottish domestic architect and interior designer, was assisted by his brother William in building the Adelphi, 1769–71.

p. 36 St John's Gate: the twelfth-century priory or hospital of St John of Jerusalem, in Clerkenwell, was the first house of the Hospitallers in England. The gateway (1504) is the only part which still survives.

p. 37 to gloom: to frown, appear darkly.

p. 38 Strasburg: Alsace-Lorraine had been ceded by France to Germany after the Franco-Prussian War of 1870, during which Strasburg was besieged and extensively damaged. The Prussian rebuildings, including the Palais du Rhin (1889), which Ford mentions, contrasted unfavourably with older French buildings like the eighteenth-century Château des Rohan (1730–42). The German side of Ford's family – the Hueffers – were Westphalians from Münster, and they had scant sympathy for Bismarck's Prussia, as is shown in Ford's own later work *When Blood is Their Argument: An Analysis of Prussian Culture* (1915). While (like his father) admiring Schopenhauer, Wagner and Nietzsche, Ford contrasted Prussian ruthlessness and efficiency unfavourably with the ethos and culture of southern Germany.

p. 38 'jerry built': a term originating in the 1870s for cheap and badly built houses, and so used by Ruskin in *Fors Clavigera* (1875).

p. 39 the Elephant: the Elephant and Castle, originally a public house in south-east London, then the name of a busy circus of converging roads nearby.

p. 39 Obelisk milestone in St George's Circus: in Southwark, erected 1771, but now moved to a neighbouring park.

p. 40 Brindley: James Brindley (1716–72), engineer, built the Bridgewater canal, the first of any importance in England, in 1759, constructing an acquaduct by which the canal was carried over the river Irwell. The Grand Union Canal, which Ford goes on to describe, can still be traced in West London, particularly at 'Little Venice'.

p. 41 wall of Hadrian: built by the Emperor Hadrian in AD 122 on the Roman frontier with Scotland to keep out the Picts and Scots.

p. 41 Horace ... the Via Flaminia: the Flaminian Way ran from Rome to Ariminum, or Rimini, on the Adriatic, and was built by Gaius Flaminius as Censor in 220 BC; but Horace does not refer to it by name in any of his poems. Is this a slip of Ford's for the Via Sacra, where Horace met the bore in *Satires* i.9?

p. 41 Carthage: the Carthaginian empire was destroyed by Rome in the First and Second Punic Wars in the third century BC.

p. 42 hanging gardens of Babylon: one of the seven wonders of the ancient world.

p. 43 Pyramid of Cheops: the Great Pyramid at Giza, a marvel of engineering skill, was built by Cheops, a pharoah of the fourth dynasty.

p. 48 Piccadilly Fountain: the Eros fountain in Piccadilly Circus (1892), designed by Sir Alfred Gilbert (1854–1934) as a memorial to Lord Shaftesbury, the Victorian social reformer.

p. 49 whether besides the Isis . . . St Andrews: i.e. whether at Oxford, which is situated at the confluence of the Isis and the Thames, or in the golfing city of St Andrews, seat of Scotland's oldest university. Ford's father had studied at Bonn.

p. 49 the sorrows of Achilles: the theme of Homer's *Iliad*.

p. 50 a city Mecca: here, a coffee shop.

p. 51 *mutatis mutandis*: with due alteration of the details of the comparison.

p. 51 Cinquecento: the sixteenth century, the great period of Italian art.

p. 52 The Holy Land: i.e. in the Crusades.

p. 52 Kaiserliks: German imperial soldiers.

p. 52 Wars of Seven, of Thirty years' duration: the Seven Years War against French influence in India and North America began in 1756. The Thirty Years War (1618–48) was waged against the designs of Spain and the German Catholic League.

p. 52 the Duke of York's column: built 1831–4, at the top of the steps down from Carlton House Terrace to St James's Park, to commemorate Frederick Augustus, Duke of York and Albany (1763–1827), second son of George III. The statue of the Duke which surmounts it is by Westmacott.

p. 52   Free Trade: the battle cry of the Liberals throughout this period, championed by Cobden and Bright, and more recently by Joseph Chamberlain (1836–1914).

p. 53   Napoleon I: one of Thomas Carlyle's modern heroes in *Heroes and Hero-Worship* (1841), echoed in the leading character of G. K. Chesterton's novel *The Napoleon of Notting Hill* (1904). The Nietzschean superman reflected a similar conception.

p. 53   the Drakes and the Raleighs ... Random's: Sir Francis Drake (?1540–96) and Sir Walter Ralegh (?1552–1618), the great Elizabethan seamen and explorers. Alessandro Cagliostro (1743–95), Sicilian charlatan and adventurer, was involved in the affair of the Diamond Necklace (1785) at the court of Louis XVI, which weakened the French monarchy on the eve of the Revolution. Roderick Random is the eponymous hero of the novel by Tobias Smollett (1721–71), published 1748.

p. 53   Macshanes ... Tom Jones: Paddy Macshane was the hero of a popular song, and Con Cregan, 'the Irish Gil Blas', the subject of a novel by Charles Lever (1849). Col. George de Lacy Evans (1787–1870) was a Peninsular officer who became something of a national hero (1838) for his part in commanding the British contingent in the Carlist Wars in Spain, but was ridiculed by Wordsworth. James Thomson (1700–48), Scottish poet, came to London to seek his fortune and published *The Seasons*, 1726–30. Tom Jones was the eponymous hero of Henry Fielding's novel, published 1749.

p. 55   Aldgate: ancient city thoroughfare near which a stretch of the Roman wall of London is preserved. The pump has long since disappeared.

p. 55   ormolu: gilded bronze used in decorating French furniture: here it suggests 'brassy' or vulgar.

p. 56   Chippendale: Thomas Chippendale (fl. 1760), the cabinet maker.

p. 56   when the war broke out: the Boer War began in 1899.

p. 56   Chinese Massacres: in the same year the Chinese rose against their German and Russian oppressors, who had occupied parts of the old Chinese empire, and the legations in Peking were besieged. Britain, which also had territorial and commercial ambitions in the area, sent an unsuccessful expedition to retrieve the situation.

p. 56 *mise en scène*: production or theatrical setting.

p. 56 **Bosnians:** shares.

p. 57 **Childs' . . . or Twinings':** Sir Francis Child, the elder (1642–1713), founded his bank in 1690 and became Lord Mayor of London eight years later. Twinings' was founded by Richard Twining (1749–1824), a director of the East India Company.

p. 57 **Swedenborg:** Emanuel Swedenborg (1688–1772), Swedish scientist and mystical thinker, was employed from 1716 on the Swedish Board of Mines where he anticipated many subsequent discoveries. From 1747 he promoted his New Church, which gained many adherents in England. He died in London, and was buried in the Swedish Church in Princes Square.

p. 58 **Nero:** the Roman Emperor, who staged a triumphant tour of Greece in AD 67, plundering the shrine of Apollo at Delphi to restore the Imperial treasury.

p. 59 **Perdita:** Mary Robinson (1758–1800), actress, mistress of the Prince Regent, later George IV (1762–1830), and author of several volumes of facile and affected verse.

p. 60 **Theocritus . . . Eastern Question:** a sweeping generalisation about the major preoccupations of the age. Theocritus, the Greek pastoral poet of the third century BC was the subject of intensive scholarly work in the nineteenth century, especially in Germany. Friedrich Wilhelm Nietzsche (1844–1900), German philosopher, was a disciple of Schopenhauer and influence on Wagner, and therefore part of the intellectual atmosphere Ford grew up in. The Eastern question refers to the recent interventions of Britain, France, Germany and Russia in the Chinese sphere of influence.

p. 62 **succeeding dominant types:** the prevalent evolutionary philosophy propagated by George Bernard Shaw (1856–1950) in plays like *Man and Superman* (1903) and *Major Barbara* (1905), and a little later in the 'creative evolution' of Henri Bergson (1859–1941), proposed in 1907.

p. 62 *caput mortuum*: worthless residue.

p. 64 **Huguenot by descent:** descended from French Protestants persecuted during the Wars of Religion in France and driven to seek asylum in England after the Revocation of the Edict of Nantes (1685).

Many settled in London as skilled craftsmen, and left a permanent mark on English society.

p. 65 Arts and Crafts: the Arts and Crafts Society was consolidated in 1887, under the leadership of William Morris (1834–96), to further good design in interior decoration. As a young man, Ford had come under his influence, absorbing the lessons of Ruskin's *Unto This Last* (1862); and his grandfather Ford Madox Brown had been an early supporter of the movement.

p. 65 *Roman d'un Jeune Homme Pauvre*: the tale of an impecunious young man, the title of a popular sentimental novel by Octave Feuillet (1821–90), published 1858.

p. 66 Cave: Edward Cave (1691–1754), printer and journalist, conducted *The Gentleman's Magazine*, 1731–54. Dr Johnson was an early contributor on parliamentary debates, 1741–4.

p. 66 footnote: Ford's sympathies lay with the old trade and craft guilds of the Middle Ages, and he deplored mass production and the giant corporations, trusts and state enterprizes that were marginalising the individual worker. His faith in the small producer is echoed in *The Heart of Country*, in his own forays into smallholding, and in *Last Post*, a rural idyll of the post-war world. It is also the subject of two of Ford's last books, *Provence* and *Great Trade Route*.

p. 69 retreat from Moscow: Napoleon's, in 1812.

p. 73 the P—: the Piccadilly Hotel?

p. 74 quarterings: coats of arms marshalled on shields to denote alliances of family with heiresses of others.

p. 76 Schopenhauer: Arthur Schopenhauer (1788–1860), the German philosopher of pessimism, whose *Parerga und Paralipomena* (1851) first won him popular recognition. Ford's father, Francis Hueffer, was a devotee of Schopenhauer, partly perhaps because of his influence on Wagner, and started the *New Quarterly Review* to propagate his philosophy.

p. 77 'going fanti': or 'fantee', to go native, after the name of a tribe in Ghana: a word popularised by Kipling.

p. 77 Savonarola: Girolamo Savonarola (1452–98), Italian preacher and reformer, established his own theocratic rule in Florence, denouncing the immoralities of the Florentines and the clergy. Excommunicated in 1497, he was hanged as a schismatic and heretic.

p. 78 Islands of the Blest: the Fortunate Isles in the western ocean, according to some classical traditions: the residence of the spirits of the blessed.

p. 80 beanfeaster: partaker of an employer's annual dinner for his workpeople (slang).

p. 81 Brahmins: Hindu priests.

p. 81 *assoupissement*: literally, drowsiness.

p. 85 Krugers ... 'A.J.B.': named after President Kruger (1825–1904), leader of the Transvaal Boers and opponent of British policy in South Africa before and during the Boer War. William II, the German Emperor or Kaiser (1859–1941), was widely regarded at this time as entertaining the dream of uniting the European states against Britain. 'A.J.B.' is Arthur James Balfour (1848–1930), Prime Minister, 1902–5.

p. 86 Khedive's interest: since the construction of the Suez Canal in 1869, Egypt had become part of the British sphere of influence against Turkish domination and in all but name a British Protectorate. The Khedive was willing to move towards a measure of home rule, but a new constitution was not published till 1913. Ford's *History of Our Own Times* offers a highly personal account of these events.

p. 86 Mark Lane: in the City, south of Fenchurch Street, no longer the name of an underground station.

p. 86 City Temple: the Congregationalist church at Holborn Viaduct.

p. 87 in Emerson ... *a bullet*: the quotation is from *English Traits*, Ch. 6, by Ralph Waldo Emerson (1803–82), the American Transcendentalist philosopher and essayist.

p. 87 the Table Talk of Shirley: reminiscences of D. G. Rossetti and other Victorian writers published by Sir John Skelton (1831–97), lawyer and author, in 1895 under the pseudonym of 'Shirley'.

p. 87 Brummel type: Beau Brummell (1778–1840) was a friend of the Prince Regent and a leader of fashion.

p. 87 the Crimea: i.e. of the period of the Crimean War (1854–6).

p. 87 Theodore Hook: (1788–1841), novelist and wit.

p. 87 Mrs Thrale-Piozzi: Hester Lynch Piozzi (1741–1821), friend of
Dr Johnson, was married against her inclinations to Henry Thrale, and
their house at Streatham became Johnson's second home. After Thrale's
death, she married (1784) Gabriel Piozzi, an Italian musician, a match
that was widely deplored at the time.

p. 89 Sunday papers: particularly the *Observer* and the *Sunday Times*,
founded respectively in 1791 and 1822. The Sunday papers, printed on
a Saturday, would contain the closing Stock Exchange prices for the
previous week.

p. 89 in Kensington: an early example, perhaps, of the increasing
evasiveness that marked Ford's recollections of his own past. The
Hueffers actually lived in Brook Green, Hammersmith, which bordered
on Kensington, but which was not quite so fashionable.

p. 91 gaffs: music-halls (slang).

p. 92 tirades of Romeo: see Shakespeare's *Romeo and Juliet*, II.ii.

p. 92 clubs: including at this date the Savile, the Naval and Military,
and the Cavalry Club.

p. 93 Nelson: Lord Nelson (d. 1805) is buried in the crypt under the
dome of St Paul's Cathedral.

p. 93 *ore rotundo*: sonorous tones.

p. 93 Happy are they . . . the worst: a parody of *Revelation*, xiv: 13,
which is used in the Burial Service in the *Book of Common Prayer*.

p. 94 Marlowe's mighty line: the elevated blank verse of Christopher
Marlowe (1564–93), praised by Ben Jonson.

p. 94 Parsees: descendants of Persians who fled to India to avoid
Mohammedan persecution.

p. 94 Kaffirs: South African Bantus.

p. 95 London 'Cemeteries': set up by a series of Acts of Parliament,
1852–1900, giving to local authorities powers to deal with the increasing overcrowding of churchyards and to regulate the manner in which
burials were carried out. Kensal Green was the first of these new
London cemeteries, established as a private company in 1832.

p. 95 Macadam: John Loudon McAdam (1756–1836), the road engineer, and inventor of the 'macadamised' road.

p. 96 Arviragus: Cymbeline's son from Shakespeare's play of that name, who took refuge in Wales.

p. 96 'R.B.K.': the Royal Borough of Kensington.

p. 97 What Socrates of London ... : What philosopher of today, Ford asks, would address his audience as 'men of London', as the Greek philosopher Socrates addressed the Athenian court at his trial as 'men of Athens'? The Greek quotation (which Ford does not cite quite accurately) is the opening of Plato's *Apology for Socrates*.

p. 97 Minneapolis: the boom city of the American Middle West, which trebled in size between 1880 and 1890.

p. 97 Helen of Troy ... Boswell: Helen, the Argive Queen, wife of King Menelaus, carried off by Priam's son Paris, and therefore the ostensible cause of the Trojan War, is conjured up in Marlowe's *Dr Faustus* as 'the face that launched a thousand ships'. James Boswell (1740–95), was Dr Johnson's biographer.

p. 98 Apollo: the Greek god of poetry and inspiration.

p. 98 Auguste Comte: (1798–1857), the French positivist philosopher, whose ideas on social evolution were influential throughout the nineteenth century: author of *Cours de Philosophie Positive* (1830–42). The quotation from Comte is inset in a dialogue in Père Lachaise cemetery, Paris, between an unnamed speaker (addressed sarcastically as 'docteur Socrate'), and Constantin Marc, perhaps from a novel by Paul Bourget (1852–1935), but not yet precisely identified.

p. 100 the Ruskins ... the Gladstones: Ruskin died in 1900, Gladstone and Bismarck in 1898, and Tennyson in 1892.

p. 103 Westminster Hall: built 1401, the only part of the old Palace of Westminster to survive the disastrous fire of 1834, but still (apart from its magnificent hammerbeam roof) considerably remodelled by Sir Charles Barry in his rebuilding programme, – which Ford goes on to denigrate.

p. 103 the young Pretender: the defeat of Charles Edward (1720–88) at Culloden in 1746 put an end to all hope for the Roman Catholic succession. But according to Ford, it also marked the final end of the old order, in that it ushered in a period of lasting peace and commercial prosperity which it was in no one's interest to disturb. Ford was already planning his trilogy *The Fifth Queen*, which depicts the clash between the Catholic Katherine Howard and Henry VIII's minister Thomas Cromwell, 'the founder of modern England'.

p. 104 Arkwrights and Kays: Sir Richard Arkwright (1732–92), inventor of the 'spinning jenny', and John Kay, inventor of the fly-shuttle (1733).

p. 104 Sir Thomas Gresham: (?1519–79), founder of the Royal Exchange and financial agent to the Crown in Elizabeth's reign. But Ford is confusing him with his father Sir Richard Gresham (?1485–1549), Lord Mayor of London and correspondent of Wolsey, who lent money to King Henry VIII.

p. 106 City of dreadful Night: the title of an apocalyptic poem by James Thomson (1834–82), published 1874.

p. 107 Conservancies: for example, the Thames and Lea Conservancy Board and the Metropolitan Water Board (1902).

p. 109 an ecclesiastical islet: Westminster Abbey was founded at Thorney, that is on the Island of Thorns, close to the marshy bank of the Thames, probably in the tenth century in the time of St Dunstan.

p. 109 Abbot Samson: Jocelin of Brakelond, a twelfth-century monk of Bury St Edmunds, wrote the life of Abbot Samson (published 1840), which formed the basis for Thomas Carlyle's *Past and Present* (1843). Carlyle's contrast between the *laissez-faire* society of his own day and the orderly community of St Edmund's Abbey in the twelfth century contributed significantly to Victorian medievalism, thereby influencing Ford's own sympathies.

p. 110 Jezebel: wife of Ahab in I *Kings*, 16, a harlot.

p. 110 Lot's wife: In *Genesis* xix:26, Lot's wife looked back on the destruction of Sodom and was turned to a pillar of salt.

p. 110 book of Job: in the *Old Testament*, preoccupied with the problem of unmerited suffering.

p. 110 Edward II: (1284–1327), an erratic monarch obsessed with Gaveston and other favourites, as in Marlowe's play of the same title.

p. 110 'Timon of Athens': nineteenth-century critics argued that in this problematic tragedy Shakespeare was either reworking a play by another or that another was reworking a play by Shakespeare. According to E. K. Chambers, Shakespeare was 'in a mood verging upon nervous breakdown' when he wrote the play. Modern scholarship now accepts that *Timon of Athens* shows no trace of any other hand but Shakespeare's, and has come to terms with the misanthropic character of the hero.

p. 110   scaramouches: braggarts (as in Italian farce).

p. 111   portraits of the loves ... of Henry VIII: Ford's early plan for a life of Henry VIII was overtaken by A. F. Pollard's biography of 1902, but much of the material he had collected was used in the *Fifth Queen* trilogy and in his monograph on *Hans Holbein*, published in the same year as *The Soul of London*.

p. 112   a cloud ... of little personal impressions: in his closing paragraphs, Ford returns to his role as the artist of impressionism, reminding the reader of his earlier aspiration that, 'Perhaps, for times to come, some individual of today, striking the imagination of posterity, may catch and preserve an entirely individual representation of the London of today'.

SUGGESTIONS FOR FURTHER READING

Ford produced eighty-one books, as well as more than 400 articles and contributions to other volumes. Only selected parts of this enormous output are ever likely to be reprinted.

The revival of interest in Ford dates from the early 1960s with the publication of Graham Greene's *Bodley Head Ford Madox Ford* (4 vols, London, 1962; Vol. 5, ed. Michael Killigrew, 1971). See Alan G. Hill, 'The Literary Career of Ford Madox Ford', *Critical Quarterly*, 5 (1963), pp. 369–79. David Dow Harvey's *Bibliography of Works and Criticism* (London, 1963), is still indispensable for its complete listing of Ford's works, as well as offering an anthology of critical reactions. A useful short biography, Frank MacShane's *The Life and Works of Ford Madox Ford* (London, 1965), was followed by Arthur Mizener's massive study *The Saddest Story, A Biography of Ford Madox Ford* (London, 1971), which is unlikely to be superseded. Other earlier studies include John A. Meixner, *Ford Madox Ford's Novels, A Critical Study* (London, 1962). *The Critical Writings of Ford Madox Ford* were edited by Frank MacShane (Nebraska, 1964), who also edited the *Critical Heritage* volume (London, 1972). See also *Ford Madox Ford, Modern Judgments*, ed. Richard A. Cassell (London, 1972).

In recent years *The Fifth Queen*, *The Good Soldier* and *Parade's End* have become available in paperback, and hardback editions of *A Call, Ladies Whose Bright Eyes* and *The Rash Act* are again in print. *The Ford Madox Ford Reader*, ed. Sondra J. Stang (London, 1986), includes poems, critical writings and reminiscences. Very little has been written about *The Soul of London* and its two sequels, but for a brief appreciation see Alan G. Hill, 'Ford Madox Ford Revisited', *PN Review*, 11 (1984), pp. 48–50. Ford's *History of Our Own Times* was published posthumously, ed. Solon Beinfeld and Sondra J. Stang (London, 1989). Among recent critical studies, consult Ann Barr Snitow, *Ford Madox Ford and the Voice of Uncertainty* (London, 1984).